# Princess Na (Volum

Ouida

**Alpha Editions**

This edition published in 2024

ISBN 9789362096395

Design and Setting By
**Alpha Editions**
www.alphaedis.com
Email - info@alphaedis.com

# Contents

# CHAPTER I.

A blue sea, some palms with their heads bound up, some hedges of cactus and aloes; some thickets of high rose-laurel, a long marble terrace shining in the sun, huge groups of geraniums not yet frost-bitten, a low white house with green shutters and wooden balconies, a châlet roof and a classical colonnade, these all—together with some entangled shrubberies, an orange orchard, and an olive wood—made up a place which was known on the French Riviera as La Jacquemerille.

What the name had meant originally nobody knew or everybody had forgotten. What La Jacquemerille had been in the beginning of time— whether a woman, a plant, a saint, a ship, a game, a shrine, or only a caprice—was not known even to tradition; but La Jacquemerille the villa was called, as, before it, had been the old windmill which had occupied the site, ere steam and fashion, revolutionising the seashores of Savoy, had caused the present pretty nonsensical, half-rustic, half-classical house to be erected on the tongue of land which ran sharply out into the midst of the blue waves, and commanded a sea view, west and east, as far as the Cape of Antibes on the one side and the Tête du Chien on the other.

It was one of the most coveted spots on the whole seaboard of our modern Capua, and brought a little fortune annually to its happy possessor, a respectable vendor of hams, cheese, and butter in the Cannebière at Marseilles, who for the coming season had pocketed now, from Prince Napraxine, the round little sum of two thousand napoleons.

And the Princess Nadège Napraxine, who had set her heart, or rather her fancy, upon it, was sitting in a bamboo rocking-chair and looking over the house front, and thinking that decidedly she did not like it. It had been an idiotcy to take it, just the sort of folly which her delegate in the affair always committed. They would have been a thousand times better off at the hotels in Nice; you had no kind of trouble at an hotel, and you could always have your own cooks if you insisted.

For three months it had been the reigning desire of her life to have La Jacquemerille for the winter; it had been let to an American millionnaire, and the apparent impossibility of getting it had naturally increased her anxiety. The American millionnaire had suddenly decided to go home; Jay Gould or Mr. Vanderbilt had done something that had disturbed his digestion, and La Jacquemerille, which she had never seen, but had fallen in love with from photographs, was granted to her wishes for the modest sum of forty thousand francs. She had travelled straight from the Krimea to it without stopping, had arrived by night, and now was looking at it for the first time in broad daylight with a sentiment very near akin to disgust. She did not find it the least like the photographs.

'It is so horridly low!' she exclaimed, after a long and thoughtful examination of the frontage, where an Ionic colonnade sheltered itself under a châlet roof from the Bernese Oberland. 'I am sure it will be most dreadfully cold. And just look at the architecture—every style under heaven! Was there ever such an extraordinary jumble?'

'If it be a jumble, my dear, it is very suitable to our generation; and you are very lucky if, when you buy a pig in a poke, you get nothing worse than a jumble,' said another lady who was sitting opposite to her, with a book held upside down and a litter of newspapers, and who was known in society as Lady Brancepeth.

'Pig in a poke! what is he?' said the Princess Napraxine in her pretty English, which she spoke with scarcely any foreign accent. 'The house is shocking! It is the Parthenon mixed up with a Gasthof. It is a nightmare;—and so small! I don't believe there is room for one quarter of the servants. And just look at these palms with their heads tied up as if they had neuralgia; and I am sure they may well have it, standing still in that *bise*, day and night. I think the whole place utterly odious. I will tell the women to unpack nothing; I am sure I shall not stay a night; an Italian *villino* with a shingle roof and Grindenwald balconies! Can anything be so absurd?'

'I suppose you will wait till the Prince comes downstairs?' said Lady Brancepeth with a little yawn.

'Oh, I don't know; why? He can stay if he likes. Oh, dear! there is a Cairene lattice at that end and these other windows have been copied from the Ca d'Oro, and the roof is as Swiss as if it were a cuckoo clock or a St. Bernard dog. What is one to do?'

'Stay,' suggested Lady Brancepeth. 'People do not die of a Swiss roof unless it tumbles in. The house is all wrong, no doubt, but it is picturesque; a horrible word, you will say, but it describes the place. It *is* picturesque.'

'Wrong things usually are,' said the Princess Napraxine with a sigh, as she surveyed the Greek peristyle, the Swiss shingles, and the slender Ionic colonnade. 'Are all these oranges good for one's complexion, I wonder? It is like sitting in a bright yellow room. I don't like bright yellow rooms. Who said that granted wishes are self-sown curses? Whoever did must have wished to hire La Jacquemerille, and done it. Why do they tie up those palms?'

'To blanch the leaves for Holy Week. Every blade of grass is turned into money on this poetic shore. If the gardens have been included in your agreement you can untie them; if not, you cannot.'

'They will certainly be untied; as for agreement—your brother took the place for us, I daresay he blundered.'

'What were your instructions to him, may I ask?'

'Oh, instructions? I do not remember. I sent him the photographs, and wrote under them: "Take me the house at any price."'

'Curt as Cæsar!'

With a little yawn the Princess Napraxine looked down the long shining sea-wall of white marble, studded at intervals with vases of white marble filled with aloes; beyond the marble wall was the sea—blue, bright, quivering, and full of shifting lights as diamonds are. Then her gaze came inward, and returned to the outline of the house which was so daring and contradictory a jumble. The creepers which covered it glowed red in the December noon; its blue and white awnings were gay and fresh; its vanes were gilded, and pointed merrily to the south; a late rose was garlanding the Cairene lattice; some woodlarks were singing their pretty little roundelay on the boughs of a carob tree; it was all bright, lively, full of colour and of gaiety. Nevertheless, she hardened her heart to it and condemned it utterly, out of mere waywardness.

'I shall go away after breakfast,' she said, as she looked. 'Platon can do as he likes. I shall dine at Nice, and you will come with me.'

'I was sure that was what you would do,' said her friend; 'so was Ralph.'

'Then I shall not do it,' said Princess Napraxine.

She rocked herself soothingly in her chair.

'What a dear little bird that is singing; it cannot be a nightingale in December. The sea looks very much like our Krimean one; and what a lovely air it is. Like an English June without the rain-clouds.'

'Wait till Madame la Bise comes round.'

'Oh, Madame la Bise comes round the corner everywhere. She is like ennui—ubiquitous. You have her in England, only you pretend she is good for your health, and your Kingsley wrote an ode to her; the rest of the world is not such a hypocrite.'

'Kingsley? He was *Tom Brown*, was he not?'

'You are *Tom Brown*! Really, Wilkes, you know nothing of your own literature.'

'Well, I was never educated as you clever Russians are,' said Lady Brancepeth, good-humouredly; she was sometimes called Socrates, and generally Wilkes by her intimates. She was the ugly member of a singularly handsome family, and the nickname had been given to her in the schoolroom. But her ugliness was a *belle laideur*; her face was charming in its own way; her eyes were brilliant, and her figure was matchless. She was an earl's daughter and an earl's wife, and when she put on the Brancepeth diamonds and showed herself at a State ball, if ugly she was magnificent, even as, if intellectually ignorant, she was a marvel of tact, humour, and discernment.

Her friend and hostess was as entirely unlike her as an orchid is unlike an aloe. She was exquisitely lovely, alike in face and form, and as cultured as a hothouse flower. She was just three-and-twenty years old, and was a woman of the world to her finger tips. She was very cosmopolitan, for though a Russian by birth and marriage her mother had been French, one of her grandmothers English, the other German, and she had been educated by a crowd of governesses of many different nationalities. All her people, whether Russian, English, French, or German, had been very great people, with innumerable and unimpeachable quarterings, for many generations, and to that fact she owed her slender feet, her tiny ears, and her general look of perfect distinction. She had a transparent, colourless skin, like the petals of a narcissus in its perfect *mat* whiteness; she had oriental eyes of a blue-black, which looked immensely large in her delicate face, and which could have great inquisitiveness, penetration, and sarcasm in them, but were usually only lustrous and languid; her mouth was most admirably shaped, and her teeth deserved the trite compliment of the old madrigals, for they were like pearls; she had a very ethereal and delicate appearance, but that delicacy of mould sheathed nerves of steel as a silken scabbard sheathes a damascene blade. She had an infinite grace and an intricate alternation of vivacity and languor which were irresistible. Men were madly in love with her, which sometimes diverted and sometimes bored her; many people were rather afraid of her, and this pleased her much more than anything. She had a capacity for malice.

She now held a sunshade above her head and surveyed the house, and tried to persuade herself it was charming, as her friend had been so sure she would find it detestable. She had wished for the place with an intensity that had almost disturbed her sleep for some weeks, and now she had got it and she hated it. But as they had expected her to do so she was determined to conquer her hatred and to find it much better than its photographs. The task was not difficult, for La Jacquemerille, if full of absurdities and incongruities, was decidedly pretty.

As she swung herself on her rocking-chair and began to see with the eyes of her mind a hundred improvements which she would instantly have effected whether the terms of the contract allowed of it or not, she saw coming within the range of her unassisted eyesight a large and stately schooner, with canvas white as snow bellying in the breeze. She drew on her long loose tan-coloured glove cheerfully, and said aloud:

'After all, it is better than an hotel. There is no noise, and nobody to stare at one. I daresay we shall get through three months without cutting each other's throats.'

Lady Brancepeth turned and looked out to sea, and saw the schooner, and smiled discreetly; she said as discreetly:

'I am so glad, dear, you won't fret yourself too much about the place; after all, you are not going to live in it for a lifetime; and though, no doubt, it is utterly wrong, and would give Oscar Wilde a sick headache, yet one must confess it is pretty and suits the sunshine.'

The trees had been cut, so that openings in their boughs allowed the sea to be seen from any point of the terrace. Princess Nadine from under her sunshade watched the stately yacht draw nearer and nearer over the shining path of the waters, and drop anchor some half mile off the shore; then she saw a gig lowered, with red-capped white-shirted sailors to man it, and a figure which she recognised descended over the schooner's side into the stern of the boat, which thereupon left the vessel, and was pulled straight towards La Jacquemerille. Neither she nor Lady Brancepeth appeared to notice it; they talked *chiffons*, and read their newspapers; but the long boat came nearer and nearer, until the beat of the oars sounded directly under the walls of La Jacquemerille, and the rowers were too close at hand to be seen. But the Princess Nadine heard the rattle of the oars in the rowlocks, the shock of its keel against the sea stairs below, which she could not see for the tangle of pyracanthus and mahonia and many another evergreen shrub, covering the space between the terrace and the shore; she heard a step that she knew very well, the sound of which moved her to a slight sense of anticipated amusement, and a stronger sense of approaching weariness, and she turned her head a little, with a gracious if indifferent welcome in her eyes, as a man ran up the stairs at the end of the terrace, and came along the marble floor in the sunshine—a young man, tall, fair, athletic, with a high-bred look and handsome aquiline features.

'You have had a very quick run, surely?' said the Princess Napraxine, stretching out her tan glove.

'Well, we did all we knew, and crammed on every stitch we had,' the new comer answered, as he kissed the tips of the glove, and murmured in a lower tone, 'Were you not here?'

Then he crossed over to where Lady Brancepeth sat, and kissed her cheek with a brother's indifference.

'Dear Wilkes, are you all right?' he said as he took up a majolica stool and seated himself between them.

'Take that bamboo chair, Geraldine,' asked the Princess. 'That china stool does not suit your long legs at all. How many hours really have you been coming from Genoa? I am fearfully angry with you, by the way; how could you take this place?'

'Because you told me,' answered Lord Geraldine, staring hard. 'What was the command? Take it, *coûte que coûte*. Not an "if"; not a "perhaps"; not a "but." Wilkes, do you not call that too cruel?'

'My dear Ralph,' said Lady Brancepeth, 'any woman's instructions should always be construed so liberally that a margin is left for her at the eleventh hour to change her mind. But do not distress yourself. I do not think Mme. Napraxine really dislikes the place. It is only her way. When she has bought a thing she always finds a flaw in it. It is her habit to condemn everything. She is a pessimist from sheer want of ever having had real disappointment.'

'Look at the house. It speaks for itself,' said the Princess, contemptuously. 'Why did you not telegraph and say that it was a patchwork of every known order of architecture? I would have told you to break off negotiations.'

'But you had seen the photographs.'

'Photographs! Would you know your own mother from a photograph if you had not been told beforehand whose it was?'

'I am so sorry,' murmured Geraldine, as he turned round and gazed at the offending building. 'It is a pretty place, surely? not classical or severe, certainly; but cheery and picturesque. I looked all over it conscientiously, I give you my word, and it is really in very good taste inside; much better than one could have hoped for in a *maison meublée*.'

'Oh, it is Wilkes, not I, who finds it so irretrievably bad,' said the Princess Napraxine, with tranquil mendacity; 'but if it be too bad one can always go to an hotel, only in an hotel one can never sleep at night for the omnibuses, and the banging of other people's luggage, and if I do not sleep I can do nothing. Here I should fancy it is perfectly quiet?'

'Quiet as the grave, unless the sea is howling. But Monte Carlo is just behind that cliff there; with fast horses you can drive over in twenty-six minutes—I timed it by my watch. You can have a score of people to dinner every evening if you like.'

The Princess raised her eyebrows with a gesture signifying that this prospect was not one of unmitigated happiness; and Lady Brancepeth, alleging that the sun was rather too warm for her north-country bones, went away into the house, being of opinion that three was no company; her brother drew his bamboo-chair nearer his hostess, and took the tan glove with the wrist it inclosed in a tender grasp.

'So you do not like the poor place? I am truly grieved!'

She drew her hand away so dexterously that she left the loose empty glove in his fingers, and he looked foolish.

'No; I thought of going away to-morrow,' she continued, without any regard to his dejection; 'I do not like palms that have the toothache, and marble pillars that have married wooden balconies. But your sister, who always opposes me, is so certain I shall go that it is very probable I shall stop.'

'Admirable feminine logic! No doubt the poor house is utterly wrong, though it has been the desire of everybody on the Riviera ever since it was built. I felt sure you would have been more comfortable in a good hotel at Nice, and if I had ventured to volunteer an opinion, I should have said so. Wilkes is quite right; you will be bored to death here.'

'She is quite wrong; she does not like the place herself,' said Princess Napraxine, with decision, while she took back her glove peremptorily. 'I do—at least in a way. The oranges look jaundiced, and the palms rheumatic, but those are trifles. They do say it hailed yesterday, and the water in the washing-basin in the *coupé lit* was frozen last night as we came into Ventimiglia; but I saw a scorpion on the wall this morning, and heard a mosquito, so I am convinced it is the south of the poets, and am prepared for any quantity of proper impressions, only they are slow in coming to me; it is so excessively like the Krimea, terrace and all. Should not you go in and see if Platon be awake?'

'I am convinced he is asleep. It is not quite one o'clock, and you arrived in the night, didn't you?'

'Yes; but he will get up, because he will want to be off to Monte Carlo. He will spend his life there and send over expresses every hour for fresh rouleaux. When he is near a gaming-table he is so happy.'

'Enviable faculty!'

'It is my faculty too. But I try against it; he doesn't. Men never try to resist anything.'

Geraldine murmured words to the effect that his life was one long compulsory resistance, and his eyes completed the uncomplete sentences.

'Don't talk nonsense,' said his hostess. 'You know I do not like *madrigaux*; and an Englishman always looks so clumsy when he is making them. Make me a cigarette instead.'

'Always cruel!' murmured her companion, obediently rolling up Turkish tobacco.

'Always kind,' said the Princess. 'People who are kind to men and children never spoil them. Where will your schooner stay? There is no dock, or quay, or whatever you call it, here. These places always ought to have one of their own.'

'How can they when the rocks go sheer down into deep water? No, I must keep her off Villefranche or Monaco. She can be round in half an hour—at your disposition, of course, like her owner.'

'If she be not more manageable than her owner——'

'Oh, Nadine! When I only live to obey your orders, and never even receive a smile in return!'

'Ah, if you want reward there is no longer any merit! And do not call me by my name in that manner; you will do it some day before Platon.'

'He doesn't mind.'

'No, of course he does not mind; but I do, which is more to the purpose.'

'You are very unkind to-day, princess. This unhappy Jacquemerille! it is grievous that you don't like it; the gardens are really pretty, and the view is superb.'

'You talk like an auctioneer; go and find the gardener and tell him to untie those palms.'

'Pray don't send me away yet.'

'Is that what you call your docility?'

His hand stole towards hers again.

'Do tell me, princess,' he murmured timidly. 'You will stay now that you are here, will you not?'

'How can I answer for the duration of my fancies? Perhaps I may, if you amuse me well enough.'

'I would rather interest you.'

'Ah, my friend, that is quite impossible. Even to be amused is hard enough, when one is not in the humour. When one is in the humour, it is even fun to go out fishing; when one is not, one is dull even at a masked ball at Petersburg. We are like the cuttle-fish, we make our sphere muddy with our own dulness. How would you suggest that I should find any interest here? There will be no society except some gouty statesmen and some sickly women, a few yachtsmen, a pigeon-shooter or two, and quantities of people one cannot know.'

'There will be heaps of people who know you,' said Geraldine, almost with a groan; 'at least, if you deign to allow them the *entrée* of La Jacquemerille. If I might presume to advise, the place is all to itself, they cannot come if you do not invite them. It is as nearly simple nature here as a *mondaine* and an *élégante* like you can ever bring herself to go. You have the sea at your feet and the mountains at your back; you can have absolute repose and leisure unless you wilfully bring a horde of men and women from Nice and Monaco. You are so clever; you might make endless sketches. If I were you, I should make it the occasion to get away from the world a little; if the world you must have, I should take it in the Avenue Josephine instead of at La Jacquemerille.'

The Princess laughed languidly, and looked at her cigarette.

'You want a solitude *à deux*, I daresay! But you see there are Platon and Wilkes against that, not to mention my own inclinations.'

'Pray, be serious.'

'Why? When one is in the mood to be serious, one does not take a nondescript toy within five miles of Nice. I daresay you are right; a quiet life for a little while would be very wholesome, it would certainly be a novelty, but it would be beyond me. I am not a stupid woman, I am not a silly woman certainly; no, I am quite convinced I have a brain, though as for a soul, I don't know, and I am afraid I don't very much care. A brain, however, I have; Wilkes is even unkind enough to call me learned. But still, my dear Ralph, I am, as you observed, that much-abused animal, a *mondaine*. When once we belong to the world can we ever get rid of the world? *Jamais! au grand jamais!* If we try to drink spring water, we put it somehow or other in a liqueur glass. If we smell at a hedge-rose, somehow or other Piver has got in it before us, and given it the scent of a sachet.'

'You are very witty, but——'

'I don't care in the least for "buts," and I have no pretensions to wit; I leave wit and whist to the dowagers. No; when we are once of the world worldly, we never get rid of the world again. It is our old man of the sea pickaback with us for ever? Who can lead a meditative life that dines twice a day, as we all practically do, and eats of twenty services? When we prattle about nature, and quote Matthew Arnold, we are as artificial as the ribboned shepherdesses of Trianon; and what we call our high art is only just another sort of jargon. Suppose I followed your recipe and tried living quietly here, which means asking nobody to dinner, what would happen? Wilkes would go away, Platon would sulk or do worse, and you and I should yawn in each other's faces. It is not that I have no brain, I have even a soul—if anybody has—but I began the other way, you know. It is like taking chloral; if once you do it you cannot leave off. Society is entirely like chloral; it gives you pleasant titillations at first and just the same *morne* depression afterwards, and yet you cannot do without it.'

'I hope you do without chloral; wait another twenty years at any rate before you poison yourself.'

'Twenty years! I wonder what we shall be like by then? I daresay I shall be an incurable hypochondriac, and you will have several tall boys at Eton. Perhaps your son will be falling in love with my daughter, and you and I shall be quarrelling about the settlements.'

'Nadine!'

He drew his chair very near indeed, and looked straight into her eyes. The Princess looked up at the blue sky, serenely indifferent.

'That is all nonsense, you know,' she said, with a little affected asperity, but she smiled even if she felt more inclined to yawn. At that moment there issued from one of the many glass doors of the nondescript house her husband, Platon Nicholaivitch Napraxine.

'My dear Ralph, I am very glad to see you,' he said cordially, in the tongue of the boulevards, which every gently born Russian has taken as his own. 'You came round in your "tub," as you call her? You have found the Princess dissatisfied with the house? She is always dissatisfied with everything, alas! The house is well enough; the bathrooms are small, and there is no billiard-room; but otherwise I see no defect. Breakfast is waiting and Lady Brancepeth also. Will you come?'

His wife rose languidly, and taking the arm of Lord Geraldine, drew her skirts of India muslin, Flemish lace, and primrose satin, over the marble pavement of the terrace to the house. Prince Napraxine stood a moment with his cigar in his mouth, looking south and east over the sparkling sea, then, with his hands in his pockets, sauntered also towards the house.

He was a tall, loosely-built man, with an ugly and frankly Kalmuck face, redeemed by an expression of extreme good humour; he was about thirty years of age, and had the air of a person who had always done what he chose, and had always been obeyed when he spoke; but this air changed curiously whenever he looked at his wife; he had then the timid and almost supplicating expression of a big dog, anxious to please, but afraid to offend.

'Let us go and eat Milo's red mullets,' she said now.

'Milo? Is that the cook? Can he do a *bouillabaisse*, I wonder?' he replied.

Their *chef* had been taken ill, as the train had touched Bordighera, and their agent had hastily supplied his place so far as it is ever possible to supply that of a great and almost perfect creature experienced in all the peculiarities and caprices in taste of those to whom his art is consecrated.

The Princess took no notice of her lord's blunder; indeed, she seldom answered his remarks at any time; she drew her primrose satin and soft muslin over the sill of the French window, and seated herself at an oval table, gay with fine china, with flowers and fruit, and with a Venice point lace border to its table cloth, which was strewn with Parma violets and the petals of orange-blossoms. She had Geraldine on her right hand and her back to the light. She had an ermine bag holding a silver globe of warm water for her feet, and a chair that was the perfection of ease. The dining-room was small, but very pretty, with game and autumn flowers painted on its panels, and shutters, with hangings of olive velvet and cornices of dead gold, and on the ceiling a hunting scene of Fontainebleau *à la* Henri IV.

She began to think seriously that after all La Jacquemerille would do very well for the winter. It was utterly absurd, to be sure, outside, but it was comfortable within; and, indeed, had considerable taste displayed in it, the American having wisely mistrusted his own tendencies and left the whole arrangement to French artists, who had robbed him ruthlessly, but who had made each of his apartments as perfect in its way as a Karl Theodor plate.

'I think I shall buy it,' said the Princess to her companions; indifferent to her own inconsistencies.

'Wait a little,' said Lady Brancepeth. 'Don't rush from hatred to adoration. There may be all sorts of things the matter with the drains. The *calorifères* may be wrong. The cellars may be damp. The windows may rattle. The kitchens may be too far or too near. At the end of the winter you will know all its defects and all its virtues. Houses are like friendships, there is hardly one in a thousand worth a long lease.'

'Wilkes is always cynical,' said her brother.

'And nobody is a stauncher friend,' said the Princess. 'Why will she make herself out a cynic?'

'A cynic? Because I am prudent?' said Lady Brancepeth. 'If you sigh all the winter because the house is not yours you will enjoy it. If you buy it you will discover that it is uninhabitable at once.'

'Nadine is never long pleased,' said her husband.

'What does Matthew Arnold say?' answered the Princess, 'that the poet is never happy, because in nature he wants the world, and in the world he longs for nature. Now, I am not a poet, but still I am a little like that. What you are pleased to call my discontent is a certain restless sensation that our life—which we think the only life—is a very ridiculous one; and yet I am quite incapable of leading any other—for more than a week. I remember, Geraldine, that you remarked once that it was this fool of a world which makes fools of us all. There was a profound truth in the not very elegant speech.'

'I don't remember saying it; but it is certainly true. We grow up in the world as a Chinese child grows up in the jar which is to make a dwarf of him. The jar checks our development *malgré nous*. We cannot be giants, if we would.'

'I am sure it would not suit you to be a giant, Ralph,' said his sister. 'You would never like to release distressed damsels and slay disagreeable dragons. The uttermost you would ever do to the very biggest dragon would be to turn an epigram on his odd appearance. Giants are always very busy people, and you are so lazy——'

'That is the fault of the jar,' said Geraldine.

'Some people break the jar and get out of it,' said his sister.

'No, nobody does,' said the Princess Napraxine. 'You mistake there, Wilkes. The world is with us always, and we cannot get rid of it.'

The frank eyes of Geraldine conveyed to her eloquently his conviction that the discontent she spoke of was solely due to her determined banishment of one sentiment out of her life. She gave him an enigmatical little smile of comprehension and disbelief combined, and continued to unroll her philosophies—or what did duty as such.

'Do you not know the kind of feeling I mean? When we are among the orchids in the conservatories we want to go and gather damp primroses. Do you not remember that queen who, when she heard the gipsies singing under her windows, all in a moment longed to go with them? There is something of the gipsy in everybody—in everybody who has a soul. The time comes when one is tired of the trumpery and folly of it all—the wicked expenditure, the dense selfishness and indifference, the people that call themselves leaders of good taste, and yet like *foie gras* and the *Concours hippique* and *Kümmel* and *Londrès*, and the atmosphere of Paris theatres.'

'Interesting, but discursive,' murmured Lady Brancepeth. 'Primroses—gipsies—a soul—I do not see the connection.'

'You know what I mean,' said her hostess, who always expected to be understood. 'Our life is silly, it is tiresome, it is entirely selfish, it is even, in a way, monstrous; and yet we cannot live any other. We are dominated by the Frankenstein of pleasure which we have been pleased to create. When we wish to get away we cannot; we are like the queen at the palace windows—we would fain go to the greenwood, and the brook, and the fresh winds, but we cannot, because we are fastened in our gilded chair; there is always our household to shut the window and send the gipsies away. Do we ever get rid of the household, of the *galerie*, of the routine, of the infinite ennui? I am only twenty-three years old, as you all know, and I feel as if I had lived fifty years. Why? Because it is all over-full, tiresome, high-pressure; and the worst of it is that I could lead no other life if I tried!'

'I am not sure of that,' said Lady Brancepeth. 'Marie Antoinette would never have believed that she could mend clothes and darn stockings had not the days of darkness come. In those days it was just the dainty perfumed *mignonnes* like you, my dear, who were the bravest and handiest in bearing their troubles and earning their bread.'

'One never knows till one is tried,' said Princess Nadine. 'If they would begin to guillotine us I daresay we should know how to behave; dynamite doesn't do much for us. When one goes into the air without warning in little bits, in company with the plaster of the ceiling, or the skin of the carriage horses, or the stuffing of the railway carriage, there is not much room for heroism.'

'I am not sure there is no heroism,' said Geraldine. 'The certainty of the guillotine must have been much easier to bear than the uncertainty in which you all dwell in Russia—the perpetual spectre always behind your chairs, beside your pillows, under the roses in your gardens——'

'Oh, my dear Geraldine, is not death with us always everywhere? May we not kill ourselves every moment we walk downstairs, or eat a mullet like this, or start on a journey, or read a book by a night-lamp? You all wonder how Russians can exist with assassination always keeping step with them, but in reality is it so much worse than the way in which all humanity loves and laughs, and toils and moils, and makes leases for ninety-nine years, and contracts foreign loans for payment in a century, with death hanging over the whole thing ready to swoop down at any minute? If the world realised it of course it would go mad *en masse*, but it doesn't realise it though hundreds of people die every second.'

'Did Nadine ever tell you what she did last year?' said Prince Napraxine. 'She saw by chance a queer-looking can which had been placed by some of those miscreants in a niche of the garden wall of our house in Petersburg; the thing looked suspicious to her, and it had a coil of tubing attached to it. She took the whole affair up and dropped it into the fountain. She forgot to mention it till the next morning. Then when we fished it out, and the chemists reported on it, it appeared that the can was really full of nitro-glycerine as she had fancied. I think that was quite as courageous as going to the guillotine.'

'Oh, no, my dear Platon!' said his wife, with some annoyance. 'Nothing you have no time to think about is really courageous. The can was suspicious and the children were playing near it, so I thought the fountain was the safest place; it *might* have been only milk, you know. Pray do not let us attempt to compete with those people of '89. We shall fail dismally.'

Geraldine looked up with a startled apprehension in his eyes.

'Good heavens, do you mean it? Has she actually been—been—in such awful danger as that, and never told me?'

'We were all in the same danger,' said Prince Napraxine, a little drily; 'but the Princess alone had the *beau rôle* out of it.'

'Who put the can there?'

'Oh, how should I know. The police never traced it. I do not suppose it was any special design against us as individuals; only as items of a detested whole. And two of the Grand Dukes were coming to breakfast with us that day.'

'What a fuss about an ugly little tin can!' said his wife. 'The really courageous person must have been the person who brought it there; misguided, perhaps, but certainly courageous. To drive through a city in a droschky embracing certain annihilation, in the form of a little tin pot held on your knee, is a combination of absolute awfulness and grotesque bathos, which must try all one's nerves without any compensating sense of grandeur in it. A jolt of the wheel over a stone and away you fly into the air, a blurred nothing in a stream of blood and dust! No; I respect the Nihilists when I think of all they risk for a purely abstract idea without any sort of personal hope or triumph.'

'They have hatred,' said Lady Brancepeth; 'I think you forget what an invigorating, self-sustaining, all-compensating sentiment that is. Its ecstasy is its own reward. You underrate, too, the immense fascination of the power to destroy; *on se grise* with that sense of holding the annihilation of a whole community in their hands. What made the Roman Emperors mad,—the unlimited power of destruction,—now intoxicates the mechanic or the clerk who has the task of planting a can of nitro-glycerine. When statesmen, and even philosophers, theorise about human nature and all its disorders, they never give weight enough to the tremendous attraction which pure destruction alone exercises over so many minds.'

'But they have love, too; love of the poor and of a lofty ideal,' said the Princess. 'Myself, I forgive their little tin cans, though they are extremely unpleasant, when I think of their impersonal devotion. All I wish is, that their warfare was not conducted by tin cans; the thing has a ludicrous, comical, vulgar side; death dropped in a little box labelled "glass, with care"! There is no dignity in it, no grace. Pallida Mors should not crouch under a cab-cushion!'

'How can you make a jest———' began Prince Napraxine. She interrupted him:

'I am not in the least jesting, I am entirely in earnest. I do not like being made war on by chemists; I do not like annihilation left in a paper parcel; it makes one feel absurd, fate seems trifling with one. A Jacquerie hewing at one with their scythes one would know what to do with, but who can extract any Sophoclean tragedy from a Thanatus that looks exactly like a box of sardines or a pot of *foie gras*? It is not the war that I object to, it is the form it takes; and our great, grim, ghostly Russia should evolve out of her soul of ice something much more in consonance with her. Beside the burning of Moscow, the little tin cans and the burrowing like moles underground are commonplace and a little vulgar. Russia is so awful in herself. One thinks of the frozen world of the Inferno, and Dante and Virgil walking in the spectral silence; and then, after all, in hard fact there is nothing but the police, and the drunken moujik, and the man who carries his nitro-glycerine as a baker's boy carries his rolls of bread! It is bathos.'

'One never knows what you mean, Nadine,' murmured her husband. 'If you talk so at Petersburg they will think you are a Nihilist at heart.'

'I imagine half the *noblesse* are,' said the Princess. 'The *noblesse* have always dug their own graves before all revolutions everywhere. They call it "going with the times." They did it in France, they are now doing it in England, they are doing it (more secretly) in Russia. No one should forsake their order; it is a kind of desertion, like that of a soldier who runs away before the enemy. That is why I like the party obedience of your country, Wilkes; it is entirely unintelligent and profoundly immoral; to a generally intellectual nation it would be impossible, but it is loyal. I think when one has to choose between a crime and a disloyalty one must take the crime as the lesser evil of the two.'

'Voting for party is a crime very often,' said Geraldine. 'It is one of the many things as to which I have never made up my mind. Ought one to sacrifice the country to what one believes a bad measure for the sheer sake of keeping one's party in office? Surely not.'

'You solve your doubts by having no party, and never going into the Lords.'

'At least, I can do no mischief.'

'Are you certain of that?' said his sister. 'I think you place voting for party on too low a plane. If we believe, generally, that one party—say it is Conservative, say it is Liberal—is necessary to the preservation or the progress of the nation, then I think we are bound to do our best to keep it at the helm of the vessel of the nation, even if in certain minor matters we are not always in accord with the course it takes.'

'Admirably reasoned; but are not politicians always as great sophists as priests?'

'Sophists! always that cruel charge,' said a mellow and manly voice, as there entered the dining-room a person of handsome and stately presence, in a picturesque costume, with knee breeches and buckled shoes, whom the servant announced as Monsignore Melville. He was welcomed by all with cordiality and delight, and the Princess bade him draw his chair beside her, though he alleged that he had breakfasted.

'I came to see if you had arrived,' he said, as he seated himself. 'Princess, I hope La Jacquemerille is fortunate enough to please you?'

'I have been abusing it; it is a very ridiculous house, but it grows upon one; and if you will come often enough, Monsignore—— No, I never make compliments. You know you are a delightful companion, and of how many people can one say that?'

Monsignore Melville bowed low.

'You are too enchantingly kind. But all are not so kind. Lord Geraldine was accusing priests of sophism. What was he saying?'

'He was saying that politicians are the sophists, and Wilkes the head of them.'

'Because I defended "voting straight,"' said Lady Brancepeth. 'Is it not the very root and essence of English constitutional life? Monsignore Melville, who is an Englishman, will, I am sure, say so.'

'To serve the Church is only a superior kind of voting with party,' said Geraldine.

'Do not be profane, Ralph,' said his sister. 'It does not suit you. You were created with a reverential nature, and you have endeavoured to ruin it, as most men always do try to destroy what is best in them. Monsignore, answer me, is it not the highest morality to vote straight?'

'That is a very unlimited laudation, Lady Brancepeth,' returned Melville, with a charming smile. 'I should be scarcely prepared to go so far, though I am aware that there is no salvation outside such morality in the political creed of our country.'

'Ecclesiastics have no country, my dear Monsignore,' said the Princess Napraxine, 'except a heavenly one. What a comfort that must be! Platon is always being worried to return to the *mater patria*, and his conscience is so peculiarly constituted that it will never allow him to admit how intensely he hates it. As if life were not tiresome enough in itself, without everyone being burdened with the obligation to like, or pretend that they like, their country, their relatives, their children, and their church!——.'

Napraxine looked distressed:

'You have liked Russia, too, sometimes,' he said wistfully; 'and poor little Sachs and Mitz!'

His wife cast upon him a glance of sovereign disdain: 'There are only two things I like in Russia, they are the steppes and the wolves: that limitless expanse, stretching away to the dim grey sky on every side, and the sight of a pack of the gaunt grey beasts on the snow as one's sledge flies by; those two things give one a sensation which one does not get elsewhere. But it is monotonous, it soon ceases to move one; the wolves never attack, and the great, awful, white plain never leads to anything better than the posting-house, the samavàr, and the vodki, and the group of drunken coachmen.'

'The human interest, in a word,' suggested Melville.

Madame Napraxine smiled:

'Ah! my dear Monsignore, the human interest is quite as dull as the steppe and quite as ravenous as the wolf! How delightful it must be to be a priest to see all that raw material through rose-glasses!'

'May not the interest be in subduing the wolf?' murmured Melville. 'And even the steppe, under the fostering touch of May dews and June sunlight, will put forth blossoms. Is there no allegory there that Madame Napraxine will deign to accept?'

'You always say pretty things, in the pulpit or out of it,' she replied; 'but you cannot lend me your rose-glasses to see them through, so I fear they do not convince me. The astronomers who are now busy seeing canals in the planet Mars, would see nothing if they had not their glasses; no more would you. You see a soul in a drunken *dvornik*; that is quite as astonishing, and probably quite as imaginary, as the network of canals in Mars. Will you really eat nothing, Monsignore? Let us go out and sit under that awning there; a bath of sunshine always does one good, and you need not grudge yourself a half hour of leisure. I have no doubt you have been passing the forenoon somewhere with cholera or typhus or some other plague of this sanitary century. You know, Geraldine, that is Monsignore's way. He is S. Francis Xavier all the morning, and then turns himself inside out and becomes an Abbé *galant* for society.'

'I have not been to anything typhoid or choleraic this morning, or I should not be here to endanger your loveliness, Princess,' answered Melville. 'I have been where Poverty is—alas! where is she not?—and in our day those who wed with her regard it as a forced marriage, wholly joyless; and we cannot persuade them that there may be graciousness where she dwells if only cleanliness and content will sit down with her.'

'Oh, Monsignore, it is not only poverty that scares content, I can assure you,' said Madame Napraxine.

'If you be not content, who should be?' murmured Melville. 'With every possible gift of nature, culture, fate, and fortune showered upon you, why will you always persuade yourself, Princess, that your doubled rose-leaf mars everything? I do not believe the rose-leaf even exists!'

'I am not sure that it does, either,' replied Madame Napraxine; 'but I never remember to have felt contented in my life. Is content an intellectual quality? I doubt it. Perhaps it is a virtue; I dislike virtues.'

Melville was a sincerely pious Churchman, but even he did not dare to take up the cudgels in honour of poor virtue before this merciless speaker. He was satisfied with replying that content was not a quality which the tendencies of the waning nineteenth century were likely to foster.

'No!' said the Princess Napraxine. 'The note of our time is restlessness, and its chief attainment the increase of insanity.'

'If it did not sound too much like moralising, I should say that there was never any time in which there was so much self-indulgence and so little real rest,' said Melville, who had the sensitive fear of a man of the world of appearing to obtrude his own convictions, and to preach out of season and out of church.

'People require to have their brains and their consciences very clear and very calm to enjoy rest. It is the reward which nature reserves for her good children,' said Lady Brancepeth.

'I must be very good, then,' said Madame Napraxine with her little mysterious smile, 'for I rest absolutely. To know how to do nothing is a great secret of health and of comfort; but you must not wait till you are fatigued to do nothing, or you cannot enjoy it.'

'And I suppose you must occasionally be deaf to duty knocking at the door?'

'Duty! She should have her proper moments of audience, like the steward, the piqueur, the secretary, and other necessary and disagreeable people; that is to say, if she really exist. Monsignore Melville evidently is in the habit of listening to her.'

'I may say with Josef II., "C'est mon métier à moi,"' said Melville, with good humour. 'But believe me, Princess, it is not duty which prevents repose; it is far more often worry, the hateful familiar of all modern life. Worry takes a million forms; very often it is dressed up as pleasure, and perhaps in that shape is more distressing than in any other.'

'Yes, the age has invented nothing that does not result in worry. Only look at the torture to diplomatists from the telegrams,' replied Madame Napraxine, while she tendered him a cigar. 'In other years an ambassador had some pleasure in disentangling a delicate and intricate embroglio, some chance of making a great name by his skill in negotiation. An able man was let alone to mingle his *suaviter* and his *fortiter*, his honey and his aloes, as he thought fit; his knowledge of the country to which he was accredited was trusted to and appreciated; nowadays, telegrams rain in on him with every hour; he is allowed no initiative, no independent action; he is dictated to and interfered with by his home government, and cypher messages torture him at every step. What is the consequence? That there is scarcely a diplomatist left in Europe—they are only delegates. Where there is one, he is incessantly controlled, hindered, and annoyed, and all his counsels are disregarded. Meanwhile the world's only kind of peace is a permanent armed truce. But let us go into the garden.'

---

# CHAPTER II.

When Nadège Fedorevna, Countess Platoff, known to all her friends by the *petit nom* of Nadine, had reached her sixteenth year she had the look of a hothouse gardenia, so white was her skin and so spiritual her aspect, whilst her slender form had all the grace of a flower balancing itself on a fragile stalk in a south wind. That ethereality, that exquisite delicacy, as of something far too fair and evanescent for man's rude touch, fascinated into a timid and adoring passion a heavily-built and clumsy cuirassier of the Imperial Guard, who was also one of the greatest nobles written in the Velvet Book of Russia—Platon Nicholaivitch, head of the mighty family of Napraxine. He was eight-and-twenty years old, immeasurably rich, popular with his sovereign, a good soldier, and an exceedingly amiable man. He laid his heart and everything he possessed at the feet of this exquisite and disdainful child when he saw her at her father's embassy in Vienna one fateful April day.

She refused him without a moment of doubt; but he was persevering, greatly enamoured, and had both her parents upon his side. She was neither weak, nor very obedient; yet in time she allowed herself to be persuaded that not to accept such an alliance would be to do something supremely ridiculous. She resisted stubbornly for a while; but she was inquisitive, independent, and a little heartless.

Her mother, a woman of the world, full of tact and of wisdom, answered her objection that the Prince Napraxine was stupid, had a Kalmuck face, and was inclined to be corpulent—in a word, displeased her taste in every way—by frankly admitting these objections to be incontestable facts, but added, with persuasive equanimity, 'All you say is quite true, my child, but that sort of details does not matter, I assure you, in a question of the kind we are discussing. It would matter terribly to him if you were stupid or ugly, or inclined to be fat; but in a man—in a husband—in three months' time you will not even observe it. Indeed, in a fortnight you will be so used to him that you will not think whether he is handsome or ugly. Familiarity is a magician that is cruel to beauty, but kind to ugliness. As for being inclined to corpulence, he is very tall, he will carry it off very well; and as to gambling, he will never get to the bottom of his salt mines and ruby mines: that is the chief question. And after all, my dear Nadine, a man who will never interfere with you and never quarrel with you is a pearl seldom found amongst the husks; and when the pearl is set in gold—— I would not for worlds persuade you, my dear, to marry merely for certain worldly considerations, such as the great place and the great wealth of Platon

Nicholaivitch; but I would earnestly advise you to marry early and to marry for peace, and when peace and a colossal fortune are to be found united, it seems to me a great mistake to throw them both away. Somebody else will take them. I suppose you dream of love as all young girls do; but——'

'Not at all; I know this is only a question of marriage,' said Nadine, with that terrible sarcasm on her lovely young lips with which many things she had seen in her mother's house had armed her for the battle of life whilst she was still but a child.

She did not think about love at all; she was not romantic; she already thought it *vieux jeu*; but she had a brain above the average, and she fancied that she should like the man to whom she was given to be something great in intellectual power, not merely in the sense of millions and of rank. But a girl of sixteen, born and bred in an embassy, reared in the most brilliant cities of the world, having seen the great panorama of society pass before her eyes from her babyhood, is, however innocent in other ways, not unsophisticated enough to ignore the vast advantages of such a position and such wealth as the Prince Napraxine offered to her. Besides, her father wished passionately for the acceptance of Napraxine; he himself was deeply in debt, and knew that his constitution had the germs of a mortal disease.

'V'là, ma petite,' he said to her gravely one morning, 'je suis criblé de dettes: je peux mourir demain. C'est mieux que tu le prennes—— enfin, c'est un assez bon garçon.'

It was not an enthusiastic eulogy of his desired son-in-law, but he never spoke enthusiastically, and his child knew very well that under the negligent slight phrases there ran a keen and vivid desire, perhaps even a carking and unacknowledged care. By the end of that evening she had allowed herself to be persuaded, and in three months' time was married to Prince Napraxine, not knowing in the least what marriage was, but only regarding it as an entry into the world with unlimited jewels and the power of going to any theatres she chose. When she did know what it was, it filled her with an inexpressible disgust and melancholy. She was very young, and her temperament was composed of that mingled hauteur and spirituality in which the senses sleep silent long, sometimes for ever.

She bore two sons in the first two years of her marriage, and then considered herself free from further obligations to provide heirs for the vast Napraxine properties. Her husband had been ardently but timidly in love; when she intimated to him that their union should be restricted to going to Courts together and being seen in the same houses at discreet intervals, he suffered in his affections as well as in his pride, but he did not dare to rebel.

This lovely young woman, who was like a gardenia or a narcissus, who was not nineteen, and declared that all the caresses and obligations of love were odious to her, could strike terror and submission into the soul of the big Platon Napraxine, who stood six feet three inches, and had been no unheroic soldier in the frosty Caucasus and on the banks of Euphrates and Indus. She was unusually clever, clever by nature and culture, by intellect and insight, keenly, delicately clever, with both aptitude and appetite for learning and scholarship; and within the first twenty-four hours of her marriage, she had taken his measurement, moral and mental, with merciless accuracy, and had decided to herself that she would never do but what she chose. He was a big dog, a *bon enfant*, a good-natured, good-tempered cipher, but he was a great bore. And she put him aside out of her life altogether, except inasmuch as it was absolutely necessary to sit sometimes at the same table with him, and have his orders blaze beside her diamonds at State balls; and the friends of the Prince Napraxine envied her, of all her valuable possessions, none so much as that of her husband, whose revenues were inexhaustible, and whose good-nature and patience were equally endless.

Looking back to her seventeenth year she always admitted that her mother had judged rightly.

'Poor Platon!' she would say to herself sometimes when she thought so, with a little passing flicker of something like compunction. What had she given him in return for his great name, his enormous wealth, his magnificent gifts of all kinds, his honest devotion, and his infinite docility? Being very honest, when in self-communion of this sort, she was obliged to confess to herself—nothing. Her own money was all settled on herself; their rank had been quite equal; there were hundreds as pretty as herself, and she could not now recollect that in six years of marriage she had given him one affectionate word.

'The fault is not ours;' she would say, 'it is the institution that is so stupid. People do not know how else to manage about property, and so they invented the marriage state. But it is an altogether illogical idea, binding down two strangers side by side for ever, and it cannot be said to work well. It keeps property together, that is all; so I suppose it is good for the world; but certainly individuals suffer for it more than perhaps property is worth.'

Her two little boys were always left in the Krimea with the mother of Napraxine; they were much better there, she thought, growing up robust and healthy like two young bear cubs (which, to her eyes, they much resembled) in the pure breezes from the Black Sea. When she did see them she was always amiable to them, even thought she felt fond of them, as she did of the steppes and the wolves; but like the steppes and the wolves they were certainly most interesting in theory and at a good long distance. They were too like their father to be welcome to her. 'They have the Tartar face, and they will be just as big and just as stupid,' she thought, whenever she saw them.

When Melville, who had been long intimate with her family, told her, as he very often did, that it was her duty to have the children near her, and to interest herself in their education, she always replied: 'They are exactly like Platon; nothing I could do would make them different. They are perfectly well cared for by his mother, and brought up much better than I could do it. I was expected to give him an heir: I have given him two heirs. I do not see that anything more is required of me.'

And when Melville would fain have insisted on the usual arguments as to the obligations of maternity and education, she invariably interrupted him, and once said at full length, 'If the children were mine only and not Platon's, I could make something of them. But they are formed in his image; exceedingly good, entirely uninteresting. They will be Princes Napraxine, and so the world will adore them, though they be as stupid as mules and as ugly as hedgehogs. They do not interest me. Oh, you are shocked! Even you, the most original of Churchmen, cannot get over your prejudices. Believe me, *la voix de la Nature* does not speak to everybody. It does not say anything at all to me.'

'I will be an honest woman; it is much more *chic*,' she had said to herself in the first year of her marriage in the height of a Paris winter, as she had looked around her on society, with her brilliant indolent eyes, which saw so clearly and so far, and surveyed and appraised her contemporaries.

It would be eccentric, but distinguished. To her delicate, satirical, fastidious taste, there was a sort of vulgarity in being compromised. She did not go farther than that, or higher than that. The thing was common, was low; that was quite enough against it. Something that was half spirituality, half hauteur, made the decision easy to her. A certain chillness of temper aiding, her resolve had been kept. She had been as loyal a wife to Prince Napraxine as though she had loved him. Men did not obtain any hold on her. She flirted desperately sometimes, amused herself always, but that was all. When they tried to pass from courtiers into lovers, they found a barrier, impalpable but impassable, compounded of her indifference and her raillery, ever set between her and them. She fancied that it would be quite intolerable to her for any living being to believe himself necessary to her happiness; besides, she did not much believe in happiness. The world was pleasant enough; like a well-cushioned saloon carriage on a well-ordered line of rail; nothing more. You travelled onward, *malgré vous*, and you slept comfortably, and your ultimate destination you could not avoid; but if you escaped any great disaster by the way, and if nobody woke you with a shock, it was all you wanted. She did not believe in the possibility of any great beatitude coming to you on that very monotonous route.

She had that admirable tact coupled with that refined but unsparing insolence which daunts the world in general to silence and respect. The greatest *blagueur* on the Boulevards never dared to hint at a weakness or a concession on the part of the Princess Napraxine. And women, though they envied her bitterly, reviled her unsparingly, and shivered under the sting of her delicate impertinence or her pregnant epigram, yet were perfectly conscious that she had never shared their follies. Passion had as yet no place in her complex and delicate organism. She could not, or would not, understand why passion should not be content to amuse and worship her, just as a furnace fire may only bake a porcelain cup or call to life a gardenia blossom.

Now and then this refusal of hers to comprehend what she inspired ended in dire tragedy. Now and then some one killed himself because she had laughed. Now and then two people were silly enough to fight a duel about a glove she had dropped, or the right to take her down the stairs at the opera. But this was always lamentable and foolish in her sight; only its consequences, though she regretted them, did not alter her. If she had loved her husband her victims would have been less mortified; but they all knew very well that Platon Napraxine was no more to her than one of the chairs in her drawing-room. If she had even loved the world she lived in, her coldness would have been more intelligible; but she did not. Her magnificent jewels, her marvellous toilettes, her many beautiful houses, her power of gratifying any whim as it formed itself, the way people looked after her postillions in their blue velvet jackets, the perpetual fête of which society was made up for her, all diverted her but moderately. She was *mondaine* to the tips of her fingers, but not enthusiastically so, only so from habit—as she wore silk stockings or had rose-water in her bath.

'I have seen the whole thing since I was sixteen; how can it entertain me much?' she said to those who marvelled at her indifference. When it was objected to her that there were many who had seen it from sixteen to sixty, and yet thought nothing else worth seeing, she shrugged her shoulders. On the whole she understood the sect of the Skoptzi better; they had an ideal. What ideal had her world?

She kept her exquisite tint and her lovely eyes unspoiled by the endless late hours and the incessant excitations in which women of the *monde où l'on s'amuse* lose their youth in a year or two. She ate very simply, drank little but water, rode or drove no matter what weather, refused forty-nine out of fifty of all the invitations she received, seldom or never made any house visits, and spent many hours in perfect repose.

'Why should you go and stay in other people's houses?' she always said to her English friends, in whom this mania is more rampant than amongst any other nationality. 'Another person's house is hardly better than an hotel; indeed, very often it is worse. If you don't like the dinner-hour, you cannot change it; if you are given slow horses, you cannot complain; if you dislike your rooms, you cannot alter them; if you think the *chef* a bad one, you cannot say so; if you find all the house party bore you, you cannot get rid of them. You must pretend to eat all day long; you must pretend to feel amiable from noon to midnight; you must have all kinds of plans made for you, and submit to them; you can never read but in your own room, and, generally speaking, there is nothing in the library—if it be an English library—except Tennyson, Wordsworth, and Mr. Darwin. I cannot imagine how any reasonable being subjects herself to such a martyrdom only because somebody else finds their country place dull without people.'

She had also ingeniously established a reputation for very delicate health, which she found beyond anything useful to spare her from being bored, and to excuse her absence from any gathering which did not specially attract her.

'I have a *santé de fer*,' she said once to a friend, 'but happily I look very fragile, and physicians, if they think you wish it, will always promise you angina pectoris or tubercles on your lungs. I have an enchanting doctor in Paris—you know him, de Thiviers—he is very famous; he will shake his head over me as if I were doomed to die in ten minutes, and he frightens Platon out of his wits—he gets a great many rouleaux at the end of the season—and he and I look as grave as the two augurs, though, like the augurs, we are both longing to laugh. It is so useful to be thought very delicate, you have an excuse for everything. If at the last moment you don't wish to go anywhere, nobody can say anything if it be your health that gives way. They would never forgive me my continual absence from the Court at Petersburg, and I certainly should not receive my perpetual passport, if they did not sincerely believe in the tubercles which de Thiviers has so obligingly found for me. Do go to de Thiviers if you are quite well and want to be ill; he understands all that sort of thing so well, and he never betrays you. He has convinced Platon that I am *poitrinaire*.'

And between her reputation for a dangerous disease in her system, and her really intelligent care of her health, she had the paths of life made very smooth to her, and was infinitely freer from any genuine indisposition than might have been expected from the fragility of her aspect, and her Russian love of hot rooms and yellow tea. Still, as a great comedian will so identify himself with his part that he at times believes himself the thing which he represents, she did at times almost persuade herself, as she completely persuaded others, that she had some great constitutional delicacy to contend with, and she would play at medicine with little needles for morphia, or a few glasses of water at Baden-Baden or Ems, as she would play now and then at baccarat or roulette in her drawing-rooms.

'Nothing is so useful,' she would say in moments of confidence. 'Look at the quantity of weariness that there is in the world from which no other possible plan will set you free. Palace dinners, diplomatic banquets, great marriages, country house visits, self-invited princes, imperial coronations, royal baptisms,—you cannot refuse them; the laws of society forbid; but if you are known to be in delicate health, no one can be offended if, at the last moment, quite unexpectedly, you get a chill and must not stir out of your own room. When there is some unutterable social tedium looming on the horizon, I always telegraph for de Thiviers, and he is always equal to the occasion.'

In this, as in other matters, she arranged her life to her own satisfaction, without any kind of misgiving that this self-absorption was egotistical. Everything had combined to make her an egotist. An only child, adored by her father, admired and a little feared by her mother, whose most intimate secrets she had divined with all the keen intuition of her natural intelligence; surrounded from her earliest years by a court of dependents and servants who seemed only to live to minister to her caprices, flattered from her babyhood by all her father's friends, secretaries, and attachés, she had imbibed selfishness as inevitably as a young willow sucks in the moisture from the stream by which it grows. There was nothing in a loveless marriage and in the clumsy and irritating devotion of a man who was ardently in love with her, whilst she only viewed him with contempt and dislike, to counteract the influences of her earlier years. The whole world conspired to induce the Princess Napraxine to live only for herself.

That she occasionally had moments of supreme generosity, and a capacity seldom or never called out for heroic courage, did not alter the main fact that her life was essentially selfish. She never did anything that she did not wish to do; the great want in her existence, to herself, was that she so very seldom felt any wish for anything. When she did, she gratified it without any scruple or hesitation.

Her mind was too clear and logical for any creed to obtain any hold upon her; nominally, of course, she was of the Greek Church, and had too much good taste to create any scandal by openly separating herself from it; but her intelligence, as critical and as subtle as Voltaire's or Bolingbroke's, would no more have submitted to the bondage of religious superstition and tradition than she would have clothed her graceful person in one of the 'Décrochez-moi-ça' that hung in the windows of Paris clothes-shops. In morality, also, she did not much believe; she read Stuart Mill's plea for the utility of virtue once, and smiled as she closed the book with a mental verdict of 'non-proven.'

Pride (that pride which has been happily defined by a French writer as *pas d'orgueil, mais de la fierté*), and the delicacy of her taste, with her profound indifference, supplied the place in her of moral laws, and probably acted on her much more effectively than they would have done. Principle is but a palisade; temperament is a stone bastion.

'Les honnêtes gens m'ennuient et les mauvaises gens me déplaisent,' she was wont to say, with a frank confession of what many others have felt, and have not had the courage to say. She had no more rigidity of principle than any other person who has been reared in the midst of a witty, elegant, and corrupt society; but her perfect taste supplied the place of moral convictions, the grossness of vice offended her like a bad odour, or a staring colour; and everything loose or coarse seemed to her an affront to intelligence and to refinement.

Sometimes she almost envied the women who could plunge themselves into the hot springs of a passion, only it seemed to her vulgar; the same sort of vulgarity as swimming in public in a rose-coloured *maillot*. She could swim like an otter, but she never swam in public. The noisy and ungrateful pleasures which delight modern society seemed to her sheer imbecilities, whilst she would as soon have descended to an intrigue with her cook or her coachman as have made an amorous appointment in a private room at a café, or have mounted the stairs of a hired house to meet a Lovelace of the clubs. '*Peut-on être plus bête?*' she would say, with supreme disdain, whenever she heard of the vulgarities which usually accompany Apate and Philotes in these the waning years of the nineteenth century. She quite understood the Parisienne in 'Frou-frou' who, tempted to make an assignation, awakes to a sense of its coarseness and commonness when she finds that the temple of love is upon the third floor in the Rue du Petit Hurleur, and that the wall-paper has five-and-twenty Poniatowskys jumping into the Elster repeated on every length of it.

'In that sort of affair,' she said once, 'you must have either secrecy or a scandal; both to me seem in bad taste. And then, with the one you are at the mercy of your maid, and with the other you are at the mercy of the newspapers. To be sure,' she added, 'I cannot, perhaps, measure the force of the temptation, for I have never in my life seen any human being to meet whom I should have ever thought it worth while even to order out my *coupé.*'

Innumerable lives had done their uttermost to entwine themselves in hers and had only broken themselves helplessly on the rock of her supreme indifference, like so many ships upon icebergs. She was a *charmeresse* in the uttermost sense of that expressive word, but she was scarcely a coquette, though the most merciless coquetry might have done much less harm than she did. A coquette desires and strives to please; Nadine Napraxine fascinated other lives to hers without effort if without pity. She had one supreme end—to endeavour to amuse herself; and she had one unending appetite—that of the study of character. She so seldom succeeded in amusing herself that she came naturally to the conclusion that most characters contained no amusing elements.

'*Vous m'ennuyez!*' was her single word of explication to those whose homage she had permitted for a while only to send them adrift without a sign of compassion or contrition. To her the three words seemed entirely comprehensive. When some one more daring than the others had once ventured to remind her that he had not been quite so hateful to her only a brief while before, she had said, with some impatience, 'Can one know that a book is dull unless one looks at a few pages? It is not one's fault if it be ill-written. I cannot say why you all weary me, but if you do, it is not my fault either.'

When once they wearied her it was of no use for them by any ingenuity, subserviency, or despair, to attempt to regain her favour. Her path, like that of all great victors, was strewn with unregarded victims. Now and then her composure had been ruffled, when the fate of someone of these had roused the adverse comments of the world, and the issue of some duel or the fact of some suicide had had her name, by common consent, coupled with it. She disliked that kind of notoriety; sincerely disliked it with all the hauteur and disgust of a very proud and sensitive refinement; but it never made her change the tenor of her ways.

'If you do not like *du potin*, would it not be better—to—to—not to give rise to it?' Napraxine himself had once humbly ventured to suggest when she was excessively angered because the journals of the hour had ventured to introduce her name into their narratives of a duel ending in the death of the young Principe d'Ivrea, who had been very popular and beloved in French and Italian society.

'*Du potin!*' she had echoed. 'Why cannot you say scandal? What sense is there in slang? Give rise to it? Ivrea was a nice boy, but irascible like all Italians, and intensely vain; the least word irritated him. He chose to provoke de Prangins because de Prangins teased him, and the old man has been too strong for the young one. It is a great pity! he had a pretty face and a pretty manner, but I have no more to do with his death than the gilt arrow on the top of the house. Myself, I would much rather he had killed de Prangins.'

Napraxine had preserved a reverential silence; he knew that there was another side to the story, but he did not venture to say so.

When the jealousies, feuds, and quarrels which it amused her to excite and foment arrived at any such tragical conclusion as this with which the Duc de Prangins had disembarrassed her salons of a youth who of late had grown too presuming, she was always entirely innocent of being the cause of it. 'I always tell them to like each other,' she would say placidly; but therein they did not obey her.

She valued her power of destruction as the only possible means of her own amusement. It reconciled her to herself when she was most disposed to be discontented. Her delicate lips smiled with ineffable disdain when she saw other women *se tordant comme des folles*, as she expressed it, in their effort to secure the admiration or retain the passions of men, while she, merely lifting the cloud of her black lashes in the sunshine by the lake, or sitting still as marble in the shadow of her box at the 'Français,' could anchor down by her for ever the thoughts, the desires, the regrets, the destinies of young and old, of friend and enemy, of stranger and familiar, merely by the passive magnetism of that charm which Nature had given her.

'Marie Stuart,' she said once when she closed *Chastelard*, 'a sorceress! Pooh! They make much too much of her. She had a charm, I suppose, but she could not have known how to use it, or she would never have married either Darnley or Bothwell, and she would never have allowed herself to be beaten by Elizabeth—a grey-haired virgin and a *maîtresse femme*!'

All women seemed to her to have been very weak: Josephine humiliated at Malmaison; Marie Antoinette, on the tumbril of death; Heloise, in her cell of Paraclete; Lady Hamilton, dying of want in Calais; Lady Blessington, poor and miserable in Paris:—what was the use of 'charm' if it ended like that?

'I shall reign as long as I live,' she said to herself. 'And if I live to eighty men will be still eager to hear me talk.'

# CHAPTER III.

'This room is stifling, it is so small; and yet there are horrible draughts in it. I dare say the ridiculous walls are not an inch thick,' said the Princess Napraxine now, as she rose from the breakfast-table, and drew her delicate skirts, with their undulating waves and foam of lace, out through the glass doors and over the marble of the terrace to the sheltered nook in which she had been sitting before breakfast, where a square Smyrna carpet was placed under several cushioned lounging-chairs. It was only two o'clock, and the air was warm and full of brilliant sunshine.

'It is all in dreadful taste,' she said for the hundredth time. 'This sort of mock-Syrian scenery, mixed up with châlets, villas, and hotels, has such a look of the stage. It seems made on purpose for *maquillées* beauties, dyed and pampered gamblers, and great ladies who are received nowhere else. Places have all a physiognomy, moral as well as physical. The Riviera must have been enchanting when there was only a mule-track as wide as a ribbon between the hills and the sea from Marseilles to Genoa, but now that the moral emanations of Monte Carlo and of the *cinq heures* at all the nondescript houses, and of the baccarat groups in the clubs which are not as exclusive as they might be, have spread all along the coast like miasma, the whole thing is only a *décor de scène*, the very gardens are masquerading as Egypt, as Damascus, as Palermo. It is all *postiche*.'

'You are very cruel, madame,' murmured Melville.

'That is the only thing you can any of you find to reply when I say anything that is true!' said the Princess, with triumph.

'The de Vannes are your nearest neighbours,' suggested her husband.

'Did you mean that Cri-Cri is *bien nature*?' she said, with her little low laugh. 'I fear neither of them will contribute anything to redeem the character of the place for either *maquillage* or gambling——'

'Why would you come to it?' he asked, with all a man's stupidity.

'Why do people ever ask one why one does things?' she interrupted, irritably. 'One imagines one will like a thing; one gets it; and directly, of course, one does not like it. That is a kind of general law. Monsignore Melville will tell us, I suppose, that it is to prevent us attaching ourselves to the pleasures of this world; but as it also operates in preventing one's attaching oneself to anybody, as well as anything, I do not know that the result is as admirable as he would imagine.'

'I never said——' began Melville.

'Oh, no, but you would say if you were in the pulpit,' she replied, before he could finish his sentence. 'You would say that even *ennui* and satiety and depression have their uses if they lead the soul to heaven; but that is just what they do not do; they only lead to morphia, chloral, dyspepsia, and Karlsbad. It is quite impossible—it must be quite impossible, even for you, Monsignore—to consider Karlsbad as an antechamber to heaven!'

Melville tried to look shocked, but did not succeed well, as he was a little Rabelaisian and Montaignist at heart, and not intended by nature for a Churchman.

'What are we going to do?' said the Prince, as he stretched himself in his chair, and lighted another cigarette.

'Stay where we are,' suggested Geraldine, who desired nothing better, as a *tête-à-tête* was a favour never accorded to him twice in twenty-four hours.

'Oh, not I, indeed!' cried Napraxine, with as much alacrity as was possible beneath his heavy 'envelope of flesh.' 'I shall go to Monte Carlo. I have told them to harness. If you like to come——'

At that moment a servant brought him a card. He read what was written in pencilled lines upon it; then raised his head with a pleased exclamation.

'*Je vous le donne en mille!*' he cried. 'Nadine, who do you think is here?'

'A goose with a diseased liver, or a hundred green oysters?' said his wife, contemptuously. 'I can imagine no lesser source for so much radiance.'

The Prince, regardless of sarcasm, or tempered to endurance of it by long habit, answered placidly:

'No; it is Othmar.'

The face of Nadine Napraxine changed considerably; the most astute observer could not have decided whether annoyance or gratification was the most visible expression; her eyes lighted with a look different to the mild amusement with which she had greeted Geraldine.

'Where can he have come from?' continued her husband. 'He was in Asia a little while ago. One is always so glad to see him. He is so unlike other people. It is only you, Nadine, who do not appreciate him.'

'He is *poseur*,' said she with languor. 'But I do not know whether that is reason enough to keep him waiting at the gate?'

'I forgot,' said Napraxine. 'There is no one less *poseur*, I assure you. Clever as you are, you sometimes mistake. Grégor, beg Count Othmar to join us here.'

The servant withdrew. Princess Nadine put a large peacock fan between her and the sun; she yawned a little.

'Seven minutes for Grégor to send down to the gate, seven minutes for Othmar to come up from the gate, a minute and a half more for him to traverse the house; we have fifteen minutes and a half in which to vilify our coming friend, as modern hospitality binds us to do. Let us begin. We must be stupid indeed if we cannot kill anybody's character in a quarter of an hour.'

'There is no character to kill,' began her husband.

'Pardon me! No one can say he is characterless. He is a very marked character.'

'That was not what I meant,' said Napraxine. 'I meant that no one could say otherwise than good of him. And if there were such a one, he should not say it before me.'

Nadine Napraxine let her eye rest on her husband with a peculiar expression, half pity, half derision, which might have given him plentiful food for reflection, had he been a man who ever reflected.

'Poor Platon! He has all the antique virtues!' she said softly. 'He even thinks it necessary to defend his acquaintances behind their backs. *Quel type admirable!*'

'Why do you like Othmar, Prince?' said Geraldine, abruptly. 'I detest him.'

'Indeed?' said Napraxine, in surprise. 'You must be almost alone, then. What do you see to dislike?'

Geraldine glanced at his hostess, but she refused to accept the challenge of his regard. She was looking out to sea with a little dreamy amused smile.

'I hate all financiers,' said Geraldine, moodily and lamely. '*La grande Juiverie* is one gigantic nest of brigands; those men get everything, whilst we lose even our old acres.'

'Perhaps that is your fault,' said Prince Platon; 'and Othmar, believe me, has nothing to do with the *Juiverie*; the Othmar are pure Croats; Croats loathe Hebrews.'

'He is very fortunate, Prince, to have your admiration and your confidence,' said Geraldine, with a sarcasm, lost on the pachydermatous placidity of his host.

'I have always liked Othmar since one day, of which I will tell you when we have more time,' answered Napraxine.

'Please tell us now,' said his wife. 'I have always been curious to know the affinity between you and Othmar. It is a walrus gambling with a stag.'

'Am I the walrus? It is an awkward animal,' said her husband good-humouredly. 'No, the tale can wait; he will be here in a moment.'

'If he were an Admirable Crichton he would be detestable, if only because he is so hideously rich,' interrupted Geraldine, with sullenness, 'and the Princess has already spoken of another defect, the greatest a man can have, to my thinking; he is *poseur.*'

'Pshaw!' said the Prince. 'How? What do you mean? Othmar, I should say, never thinks of himself.'

'Oh, he is *poseur*, certainly,' said Geraldine, with an undisguised cruel exultation in the cruel epithet. 'He is a Crœsus, and he poses for simplicity; he is a financier, and he poses as a grand-seigneur; he is gorged with gold, and he poses as a Spartan on black broth. The whole life of the man is affectation. His humility is as detestable as his pride; his liberalities are as offensive as his possessions.'

'*Tiens, tiens!*' murmured Napraxine, taking his cigar out of his mouth. 'My dear friend, you are under my roof, or at least on my terrace, so I cannot quarrel with you. I can only ask you kindly to remember what I said a little while ago, and to spare me again recalling to you that Othmar also is my friend. You will understand.'

Geraldine coloured slightly, conscious of having been ill-bred, and muttered sullenly, 'I beg your pardon.' A more tart and stinging retort was on his lips to the effect that the new comer was the last man on earth whom his host should welcome, but his awe of the Princess Napraxine repressed it. She herself gave her husband a glance of more appreciation than she had ever cast on him, and said to herself, 'The walrus is the clumsiest and the stupidest of all living creatures, but it is so honest——' and said aloud:

'Verify your quotations, was the advice given by a dying don to an Oxford student. Geraldine quoted from me, but he did not stay to verify what he quoted. I spoke in haste. Othmar is a tiny trifle of a *poseur*, but it is quite unconsciously; it is the consequence of an anomalous position. All his instincts refuse to be the Samuel Bernard of his generation, and he is equally horrified at the idea of appearing as a Sidonia. If he had only ten thousand francs a year to-morrow he would be happy and charming. As it is, with his ten millions or his ten hundred millions, there is always the sense of that wall of ingots filling up the background, and keeping, as he thinks, the sunshine out of his life. Occasionally it makes him see everything yellow, like the jaundice, and to everybody else it makes him seem a colossus, which is distressing to him, as he is of ordinary stature.'

'He is even taller than I am,' said her husband.

Princess Napraxine, who had made her little speech languidly, looking at the sea, and extended full length on her Indian cane chair, said with a little smile:

'My dear, I spoke metaphorically. I did not mean to underrate your friend's centimètres. I meant merely to explain that if he do look occasionally a *poseur* it is the fault of Europe, which, ever since he was born, has persisted in worshipping him as one of the incarnations of Mammon. If he had belonged to *la grande Juiverie* he would have been much happier. Jews can swallow any amount of flattery as they can wear any number of rings. He likes neither.'

'Count Othmar,' announced Grégor, ascending the terrace steps from the gardens.

The person announced was a man of some thirty years old, with delicate and handsome features, and an expression at once gentle and cold; his height was great, and his bearing that of a *grand seigneur*. He looked weary and dissatisfied; yet his life was one of the most envied of Europe. He greeted Napraxine with warmth, the Princess with grace and ceremony; Geraldine and his sister with a rather cold courtesy.

Nadine Napraxine had flushed a little as he kissed her hand; a lovely faint flush which made her cheeks like two pale-pink sea-shells. Geraldine noticed that momentary change of colour, and thought bitterly, 'She never looked like that for *me*!'

Napraxine was not so observant; his hospitable soul was filled with the pleasure of welcoming his friend, and he felt angered with his wife because she said so indifferently:

'I wonder you did not stay amongst the Mongols, Othmar. They must be much more original than we are. They ride all day long, don't they, over deserts of grass? How enchanting! I wonder you could tear yourself away.'

'Perhaps it would have been wiser to stay,' said Othmar, with a meaning which she alone understood. 'But I fear "the world holds us" too strongly for us to be long content even with a Tartar mare and a fat sheep's tail. I am fortunate to find you all here. I came from Egypt; I saw your name in a newspaper, and could not resist driving over to La Jacquemerille.'

'You have your "Berenice"?'

'Yes; she has behaved very well; we met with a typhoon in the Indian Ocean, and were nearly lost; but she has been patched up and ran home bravely. I have left her at Marseilles to be thoroughly overhauled.'

'You will have to try her in a match with Geraldine's "Zostera."'

'I could not hope to compete with Count Othmar,' said Geraldine, sullenly; for him the skies were overcast, the sun was clouded, the pretty marble terrace with its gay awnings seemed dark with the gloom of night.

He hated La Jacquemerille which he had been so eager to persuade his friends to inhabit: who could have told that this man would drop on this Mediterranean shore without note of warning, at a moment when he was supposed to be safe on the sandy steppes of Mongolia? 'As Count Othmar never, I believe, shot anything in his life, I cannot perceive what possible attraction any wild life can have for him,' he added now, in a tone that was aggressive and impertinent.

Othmar glanced at him with a regard which said much, as he replied simply: 'I have shot the most noxious animal—man; I have never, I confess, shot wood doves or tame pheasants.'

'Geraldine will shoot doves all the week,' said the Princess, with a sense that La Jacquemerille had become interesting. She loved to see men on the brink of a quarrel: sometimes she restrained them from passing the brink; sometimes she did not; sometimes she helped them over it with a little imperceptible touch, light as the touch of a feather, which yet had all the power of electricity.

'That is modern knighthood,' said Othmar. 'I prefer my Mongols.'

'My brother is English,' said Lady Brancepeth, to avert disagreeable rejoinders; 'he always reminds me of the old French caricature: "It is a beautiful day; let us go and kill something."'

'Othmar is more English than Croat,' said Napraxine, 'but he does not kill things, he prefers to paint them.'

'*Crésus doublé de Corôt*,' murmured his wife. 'Othmar, have you sketched any Mongol ladies? are there such beings? or are they only as that terrible Dumas has it, *la femelle de l'homme*?'

'Only *la femelle de l'homme*, Madame. They cannot be said to be women in any civilised sense of that term; they only know the duties of maternity, and are ignorant of the victories of coquetry. You will perceive that they are an entirely elementary animal.'

Princess Nadine heard with a little smile; she knew what allusions to herself were contained in the words.

'You should have married one of them,' she said, slowly moving her big fan. 'It would have been too picturesque; the owner of two hundred millions dwelling by choice under a pole and a piece of blue cloth, and——'

'Cannot you forbear to quote my millions?' said Othmar. 'You would not reproach a hunchback with his hump.'

'Though it is the only thing which makes him noticeable,' muttered Geraldine, but the fear of his hostess made him speak too low to be overheard save by Othmar, who did not deign to notice the insolence.

'You think money is not interesting,' said the Princess Nadine, 'but you are wrong. It is the Haroun al Raschid of our day. It is the wand of Mercury. It is the sunshine of life. Only fancy, Othmar, if you chose you could make the desert blossom like the rose; you could call up a city like Paris in the centre of your Mongolian steppes; that is very interesting indeed. Money itself is not so, but when one considers its enormous influence, its fantastic powers, it is so; it is even more, it is positively bewitching.'

'When it comes out of anything so fairylike and invisible as the Prince's salt-crystals it may be,' replied Othmar, 'but not when it is tainted by commerce. Remember, Princess, your Mercury was the god of the mart and of the thieves.'

'That was in the Roman decadence.'

'And are we not in a decadence?'

'It is the fashion to say so, but I am not sure. Have we decayed? and, if we have, from what? The last century contained nothing noble.'

'Even the burning of Moscow belongs to this,' said Othmar, with a bow to Napraxine, whose grandfather had been one of the foremost generals at the defence of Moscow, and one of the chief counsellors of that heroic sacrifice.

'Othmar always remembers what is fine in history and in his friends,' said the Prince, well pleased. 'He is not like Nadine there.'

'No, indeed,' said Lady Brancepeth; 'she always likes to see that a great man is a little one somewhere; she will always find out the speck on the handsome rosy apple, the yellow stain on the ivory, the rift in the lute—that is her way. She would never have admired Dr. Johnson, she would have only laughed at his uncouthness and his dishes of tea, and only seen that he touched all the posts in the streets.'

'I cannot help it if I am observant, and Dr. Johnson certainly would have bored me,' said the Princess.

'Les délicats sont malheureux:

Rien ne saurait les satisfaire,'

quoted Othmar.

'Then you and I are both profoundly miserable,' said Nadine Napraxine. 'I believe we have never found anything that satisfied either of us.'

'Except, perhaps, each other,' muttered Geraldine, in a smothered voice, his jealousy conquering his prudence. It was a phrase which no one heard except his hostess, who was as quick at hearing as Fine Ears. She did not deign to take any notice of it; it could be punished at her leisure.

'What an idiot he is,' she thought; 'as if *that* tone could ever succeed with *me*!'

She had herself become amused, serene, good-tempered, immediately, that with the entrance of Othmar the twin masks of tragedy and comedy had appeared to her prescient eyes to lie upon the stage of the terrace of La Jacquemerille. The whole place changed to her: the view was beautiful, the house was quaint and full of colour and variety, the orange wood was a delightful bit of local colour, the marble colonnade and the brown wooden balconies were absurd certainly, but garlanded about with all those sweet American creepers they had a graceful effect; nowhere else in December would you get roses and geraniums and white marbles and blue waves, and a thermometer at 20° Réaumur.

Othmar had brought that dramatic element into her life without which, despite her really very high intelligence, ennui was apt to descend upon her. When his eyes encountered that look they became very cold, and had a challenge in them: the challenge of a man who defies a woman to make him again the slave of her caprices. Her husband saw nothing of those glances. Geraldine saw more even than there was to see, and became moody and dejected. He only roused himself now and then to say what he thought might be hostile or disagreeable to the new comer. His remarks were ignored by Othmar, which increased his irritation. The Princess was amused, as she was, occasionally, at a good theatre, by the sullenness of the one man and by the coldness of the other. Both had elements, perhaps, of tragedy and comedy. She felt a sudden exhilaration and increase of interest, such as a person fond of a theatre feels when the great actor of the hour makes his entry on the scene. Geraldine was very useful, she had known him several years: he was always hopelessly in love with her, timid, devoted, and obedient; but he had no originality of character to make him very interesting. He was extremely good-looking, very popular, and very amiable, but he was commonplace; he had not the wit of his sister. She had admitted him into her intimacy because he was humble, handsome, and usually so docile that he seldom irritated her, but he gave no interest to her life whatever; whereas Othmar—she had scarcely ever confessed it even to herself—but whilst Othmar had been lost to sight in the wilds of Asia, society had seemed to her even more stupid than usual.

One had been in love with her for a year; the other two years before had loved her. There was a considerable difference in the two passions, which she, with her analytical mind, could perfectly appraise.

For the one she was quite sure of her sentiment in return. He was good-looking, agreeable, useful, submissive; he diverted her sometimes, wearied her occasionally, obeyed her always. She liked him, and liked better still to tease him. The other had brought into her life a sense of a stormier emotion than she cared to raise. He had been more in earnest than she chose to allow; he had loved her imperiously, ardently, unreasonably; when she had made light of it, he had left her with indignation and scorn. He had been one of those who had fought a duel about her, though none but himself and his adversary had ever known that she was the cause of it, a card at *écarté* having served as the colourable pretext. She had never been quite sure what she had felt for him; admiration in a way, perhaps, but more, she thought, dislike. But his had been one of the conquests which had most flattered her. When he had left all his habits and friends and possessions to plunge into Asian solitudes, she had felt that her power over him was illimitable. And now he had returned and told her, with as much chill assertion as a regard could convey, that her power existed no more for him. She did not care, but the change interested her, and piqued her.

'Poor Othmar!' she had said often to herself, when remembering the passages which had passed between them, and thinking of him in Asia; and now he was back from Asia, and sitting on her garden-terrace at La Jacquemerille, and was telling her by manner and by glance—perhaps telling her too persistently and insistantly for it to be entirely true—that he had vanquished his madness.

It had been a strong if short-lived madness, born first in a country-house in the Ardennes, in autumn-woods and tapestried galleries and the stately revelries of a Legitimist party of pleasure, fanned by her own will into flame in the course of a brilliant, giddy, insensate winter season in Paris. Then with spring had come the decisive moment when he had declined to be content any longer with his position, and he had been lightly laughed at, disdainfully jested with; and had revolted, and had gone out of Europe after a duel which had made even her tranquil pulses beat a little quickly in apprehension of the possible issue.

With her usual consummate tact she had so borne herself that the six or eight months' devotion, in which Othmar had been the shadow of her every step, had attracted no injurious notice from her husband or her world. It was known that he was passionately attached to her, but so many were so also, that beyond a little more attention than usual, because he was a more conspicuous person than most, the great world of Paris only smiled and watched to see if the snowflake melted. It did not melt, and he went to Asia. The duel had only come out of a trivial dispute at a club, so every one believed, Prince Napraxine as innocently as the rest.

It was after the departure of Othmar that her society took to naming her the *flocon de neige*. It seemed strange, both to men and women, that Othmar should have been so near her so long and have left no impression on her life. He had usually a strong influence on those whom he sought; in this instance he had been the magnetised, not the magnetiser.

Men always quoted Princess Nadine to their wives as an example to be followed for the serene indifference with which she flirted all the year through, yet never was compromised by a breath of calumny. Their wives sometimes retorted that she had no heart, so could not lose it.

'I promise you I will never be compromised,' she had said to her father a few months after her marriage; and he, a very easy and philosophic man of the world, had answered:

'I am sure you mean what you say; but the test of your resolution will come whenever you shall meet the person who pleases you. At present you laugh at them all.'

'I do not think I shall ever care,' she had said, with much accurate knowledge of herself.

Othmar, momentarily lava, had thrown himself in vain against this indifference; the ice of her temperament had not changed under the volcanic fires of his. All those airy nothings, that capricious friendship, that unrecompensed position of servitude which she offered him, he would have none of, and told her so with passion and force.

'And I will have no melodramatic passions to disturb me,' she had said. 'They are absurd. They are out of date. They are tiresome.'

Wounded and incensed, he had taken her at her word more completely and instantly than she had intended; and she had not known whether to feel regret or relief. She had felt a good deal of triumph. And now he had returned, unchanged in appearance, handsomer even for that duskier hue which the desert sun had left on the marble of his features; and she, and he himself, were silently wondering—was she glad?

He thought she was annoyed; Napraxine thought so too; Geraldine alone, with a lover's self-paining penetration, felt that life had grown sweeter and more stimulating to her, that her languid interest in existence had grown quicker of pulse and more content with its own atmosphere since her husband had read aloud the name of Othmar on the pencilled card.

Perhaps, thought he also, with a lover's self-torture, what he had found in her of indifference, of disdain, of lack of sympathy, had been due to the absence of the sole person who possessed the power to touch her dormant emotions.

In reality, Madame Napraxine at that moment felt no more than the vague expectation and gratification of a spectator at a theatre, who sees a drama complicate itself, mingled with a certain sense of curiosity as to why Othmar sought to display to her so conspicuously his escape from her sorcery. She was not mortified; she was accustomed to change her adorers into her friends, and she was of a nature too integrally proud to be capable of small things. She only wondered—and doubted a little.

Could any one who had loved her once fail to love her all his life?

She thought not. Yet she was not vain.

# CHAPTER IV.

'The "Zostera" looks tempting in the sunshine,' said Nadine Napraxine, as she rose and leaned on the marble balustrade to gaze over the sea, where the stately sailing yacht of Geraldine was at anchor outside the little bay of La Jacquemerille, which was too shallow to be entered. 'I will go out in her in ten minutes' time. I prefer to watch the sunset from the sea, and the sunset will be very fine to-day, for there are a few clouds above; the sky is usually so terribly monotonous here, it is like an eulogy of your predecessor at the Academy: *il y a trop de bleu*. Monsignore, I will take you back to Nice by the coast. I dislike coasting usually, but along this shore it is pretty, and besides, it is too late to go far out to sea. Lord Geraldine, go and give your men the order. I will go and change my clothes.—Wilkes, you will come?'

Geraldine sullenly obeyed, and went down the steps to where his long boat was still in waiting. In a very few moments the Princess Napraxine returned, not clothed in any maritime fashion, for she thought that sort of thing theatrical, foolish, and staring; but wearing a dark serge gown, fitting with marvellous precision to the perfect contour and lines of her form, and carrying a scarlet parasol large enough to shelter the dignity of any Chinese mandarin. She wore yachting shoes and scarlet stockings; her feet, like her hands, were such as sculptors dream of but seldom see.

'Tell them to put in my furs,' she said to Geraldine. 'Are you ready? It is always so cold here when the sun has gone down. We will take Count Othmar and Monsignore Melville to Nice. It is a beautiful day for a sail, just wind enough and not too much. Platon goes to his adored *tripot*; I wonder he stayed to eat his breakfast.'

'The "Zostera," of course, is at your commands,' murmured Geraldine, with ill-disguised ill-humour. 'For myself, if you will excuse me, I will accompany the Prince.'

She smiled, understanding his ill-humour well enough.

'How immoral they are!' she said to Melville. 'The *salle de jeu* by daylight is monstrous; but since it is their form of happiness——'

'Happiness!' muttered Geraldine between his teeth.

'All your preaching and mine will not alter them,' she continued. 'It is an extraordinary thing; neither Platon nor Lord Geraldine cares a straw for money; neither of them would awake a whit merrier if their fortunes were quadrupled to-morrow; and yet they find absolute intoxication in playing for money! What an inexplicable anomaly! Othmar is far more consistent. He despises his own fortune and the table of M. Blanc with equal sincerity.'

'I do not despise wealth, I dislike it,' said Othmar.

'Why should you do either?' said Melville. 'Look at the immense potentialities of great riches.'

'That is what I said this morning,' continued Princess Nadine.

'Surely great riches help one very nearly to happiness,' continued Melville. 'I do not mean from the *bourgeois* point of view, but simply because they remove so many material obstacles in the way of happiness. There can be hardly any great difficulties for a very rich man. He goes where he chooses, he can purchase whatever he desires; there are swept aside from his path for ever all the thousand and one annoyances and hindrances which beset the man who is not rich. Only imagine a person who cannot reach his dying child because he has not money enough for the journey; imagine another who has his homestead made intolerable to him by the erection of a steam-mill, and yet is obliged to end his days in it because he cannot afford to move; imagine yet another with weak lungs, who would recover his strength if he could take a house in the country, in the south, and yet cannot leave his business, which chains him to a city in the north. Those are the sort of sorrows from which wealth sets free a man or a woman. One may say roughly, I think, that if his health be good, a very rich person is exempt from all other misfortunes than those which come to him from his affections or his friendships; his troubles are, in a word, entirely those of sentiment.'

'Precisely,' said Nadine Napraxine.

'Un seul être est mort et tout est dépeuplé!'

murmured Othmar; 'you will not allow, or cannot comprehend that, Princess?'

'I can imagine that a man might fancy so for twenty-four hours; but even if the fancy endure, a rich man can enjoy his desolation while a poor man cannot. Part of the advantages of the rich man consists in his having the leisure and the luxury to muse upon his own unhappiness. I think you forget what a great happiness that is!'

'You believe neither in love nor in sorrow,' said Othmar, abruptly.

'I am aware they exist, if you mean that,' she replied; 'but their existence chiefly depends upon the imagination.'

Othmar gave an impatient gesture.

'And, like all pleasures of the imagination,' she added, 'require leisure for their development. The rich man or woman enjoys that leisure, and if he or she like to raise a gigantic mushroom under glass, in the way of exaggerated affections or sentimental regrets, they are at liberty to do so. Besides, surely, no one can deny that there is a captivating sense of power in vast riches; the fancy can take endless flights in that golden sphere; we do not know that delight, because, though people think us rich, in reality we are no such thing, in reality our expenses keep for ever ahead of our income, as I think they do with most people; but Othmar, who is actually, positively, fabulously rich, who is all alone, who spends nothing on himself—at least, he used to spend nothing—why, he could build you a cathedral, Monsignore Melville, in every city of the world of jasper and chalcedony, whatever they are, and never be a sou the poorer for doing it.'

'Are you inclined, Count Othmar?' said Melville.

'If it would make all men like you I should be so,' said Othmar. 'But I regret to see that the Princess Napraxine has apparently retained only one recollection of me, and that one is of my "wall of ingots," as she termed it, which appears to separate me from her sympathies.'

'Did you hear that?' she said, not very well pleased, though it was not in human power to confuse her. 'We will let those people go to Monte Carlo, and we will have a run before the wind and leave you and Monsignore at Nice.'

'But it is not my own yacht.'

'But it is mine when I am in it, and I invite you both. Come.'

Othmar hesitated till she gave him a little look, one brief fleeting look. Two years seemed to have fled away; he was again on the staircase of the Grand Opéra, she gave him her fan to carry, she had on a cloak of soft white feathers, a gardenia dropped out of her bouquet, he picked it up; in the whole glittering mass of Paris he only saw that one delicate face, pale as a narcissus, with two wonderful liquid eyes like night; and, with a sort of shock, he recollected himself, and realised that he was standing on the terrace of La Jacquemerille beside a woman whom he had vowed to put out of his life for ever and aye.

'Come!' said Princess Nadine, and he did not resist her.

He followed in her shadow down the flight of marble steps leading to the sea; while Geraldine, with a tempestuous rage stifled in his heart, drove Napraxine (who never drove himself), as furiously as Russian horses can be driven, along the sunny road, shaded with olives and caruba trees, which led from La Jacquemerille to the gambler's paradise a few miles westward on the shore.

'When boys sulk, they should always be punished,' thought the Princess Nadine with silent diversion, as she heard the plunge and rush of the horses on the other side of the gardens, and divined that their driver was already repenting of the moment of petulance and of jealousy in which he had exiled himself from her presence, and condemned himself to the society of her lord.

'Poor Platon is the dullest of companions, and Geraldine thinks it *dans son rôle* to detest him; and yet he goes with him by way of showing his pique against Othmar. How stupid, how intensely stupid!' she thought, with exceeding amusement to herself, as she descended the water-stairs and stepped into Geraldine's boat.

It was droll to her that anybody should either detest or envy her husband, he was so infinitesimally little in her own life. She readily did justice to his good humour, his loyalty, his courage, and his honesty; but those qualities were all obscured by his dulness and heaviness, and also by the simple fact that he was her husband, as the good points in a landscape are blotted out by a fog. 'Dogs' virtues! all of them,' she called them, with a mixture of esteem and impatience, of appreciation and contempt.

The boat glided through a quarter of a mile of blue water, and brought them to the side of Geraldine's yacht, a beautiful racer-like schooner with canvas white as foam, and flying the pennon of Cowes.

'My poor "Berenice" was once as elegant and spotless as this,' said Othmar, 'but she has been through sore stress of weather. Her sails are rags, her sides are battered, her rudder is gone. She made a sorry spectacle when we hove to last night, but I am attached to her. I shall not buy another yacht.'

'You always take things so seriously,' said Princess Nadine. 'A yacht is a toy like any other; when one is broken get another. Why should you be attached to a thing of teak and copper?'

'She has served me well,' he said simply. 'You do not understand attachment of any kind, Princess.'

'It is only an amiable form of prejudice. Certainly I do not understand why you should be attached to a thing made of wood and metal.'

'Or to a thing made of flesh and blood! I believe that is equally ridiculous in the eyes of Madame Napraxine,' said Othmar, with some bitterness. 'May I ask, how are your children?' he added after a pause.

'My two ugly little boys? Oh, quite well; they are never anything else. They are as strong as ponies. They are *very* ugly; they have the Tartar face, which is the ugliest in Europe; they are so like Platon that it is quite absurd.'

Othmar was silent; the words did not seem to him in her usual perfectly good taste. They did not accord with the delicate narcissus-like face of their speaker.

'I remember that you never cared for your children,' he said, and added, after a pause, 'Nor for anything that had the misfortune to love you.'

'I do not think the children love me at all,' she said, with a smile. 'Why should they? Their father they adore because he adores them. It is always *quid pro quo* in any love.'

'Not always,' said Othmar, curtly.

'Ah, you love me still,' thought Princess Nadine, without astonishment.

Aloud she said, 'It must be, or the thing is absurd, it dies a natural death, or rather, is starved to death; nothing one-sided has any strength.'

'I think you have seen many living proofs to the contrary,' he answered. 'But pride may strangle a love which is not shared; it is a violent death, but a sure one.'

'Why will men always talk of love?' she said, with some impatience. 'After all, how little place it takes up in real life! ambition, society, amusement, politics, money-making, a hundred things, take up a hundredfold more space.'

'It is not to every one the unnecessary molecule that it is to Madame Napraxine,' said Othmar. 'You have seen a glass of water touched by a single drop of quinine? It is only a drop, but it embitters the whole glassful. So do the attachments of life embitter it.'

'If you put the drop in, no doubt,' said Princess Napraxine, drily.

'Or if some one else put it in,' muttered Othmar, 'before one knows what one drinks.'

'Oh! one must never let others meddle with one, even in drinking a glass of water,' replied his tormentor. She knew very well that he meant to reproach her, but she bore the reproach lightly. If the remembrance of her embittered any man's existence it was not her fault; it was the fault of those who would not be content with adoring her as the poor people of this sea-shore adored their Madonna shut away behind a glass case.

'By the way, Othmar, have you not a villa here?' she said, suddenly remembering the fact. 'I believe you have five hundred and fifty-five houses altogether, have you not? Is there not some place near Nice that belongs to you?'

'S. Pharamond? Yes. It is where I slept last night. My father bought some olive and pine wood and built the house in the midst of them. It has a fine view seaward.'

'Then we shall be neighbours?'

'If I do not go to Paris.'

'Of course you will go to Paris, but you will go one day and come back another, like everybody else at this season; though, to be sure, I dare say you are longing for the smell of the asphalte after a cycle of Cathay?'

'No; the asphalte is not necessary to me. It is more monotonous, on the whole, than the desert.'

'Ah! you were never a Parisien *parisiennant*; you were always in revolt against something or another, though one never could understand very well what. When you condescended to our amusements, it was with the air of a man who, to please a child, plays with tin soldiers; that sort of air of contemptuous condescension has made you many enemies. There is nothing makes the world so angry as indifference to what it thinks delightful.'

'You have offended it in that way yourself, Princess.'

'Often; but not quite with your insolence. A man who prefers his library to the clubs is beyond all pardon; and, besides, I am seen everywhere where it is worth while to be seen; you are—or were—generally conspicuous by your absence.'

'I imagine the world has grown as indifferent to me as I am to it, and having forgotten has so forgiven me. I have been away eighteen months.'

'The world never forgets its rich men, my dear Othmar. It may forget its great ones. Will forget them, indeed, unless they have a drum beaten very loudly before them. You might be great, I think, if you liked; you have so many talents, so much power.'

'I might buy a kingdom the size of Morocco or Montenegro? Very likely: such sovereignty does not attract me.'

'Of course I do not mean that: you do not want to be a Prince Floristan; you do not love the race of princes well enough. But were I you I should set some great ambition before me.'

'Pardon me; you would do no such thing if you were in my position. You would feel, as I feel, the numbing influence of what you called just now the "blank wall of ingots." When you can buy men you do not estimate them highly enough either to serve or rule them. I have all I can possibly want—materially. I have no reason to seek anything.'

'Why do English nobles enter public life? They want nothing, materially, either. Some of them are of rank, also, so high in place that nothing can be added to their position.'

'God knows why they do,' said Othmar, 'except that I think the Englishman is an animal like the beaver, not happy without work. Besides, I think they imagine that they serve their country, a delusion, but an honourable one, which must make them very happy. As I have no country I cannot be attached to it.'

'You could choose one; you are allied to several.'

'That would not be the same thing. To adore the motherland one must have known no arms, no hearts but hers; no country is more than a stepmother to me.'

'You are a very much envied man, Othmar, but you are not a happy man.'

He looked her straight in the eyes.

'I have been unhappy, but I have conquered my folly. It is ingratitude to fate to be wretched while one has health and strength and no material cares to contend with.'

'All the same, you are not happy now,' she thought, but she said, with her sweetest smile, 'You admit that you have all you want materially; all the rest is a dream, not worth keeping awake about for one hour. By the way, as you speak of countries—you are French now by law, I think?'

'My grandfather was naturalised for his own interests, as you know; but our people were Croat peasants.'

'I know I have heard you always say so; but I believe it is a fable. *You* do not come from any peasantry; besides, surely Sclavonia is old enough and dim enough to give you any mystical heroic ancestry you may prefer.'

'They might be robbers,' said Othmar, 'I do not know. There is not much to choose.'

'Everybody who is noble comes from robbers of some sort,' said Princess Napraxine; 'what were the Hohenstauffen, the Hohenzollern, the Habsburg, the Grimaldi, the Montefeltro, the Colonna? Robbers all, sitting on high in their fortresses, and swooping down like hawks on the fords, on the highways, on the moorlands, on the forests, on the little towns below them. You may be quite sure that is what your people did in Croatia.'

'You are very kind to try and console me,' said Othmar. 'Nobility, I think, consists in being able to trace the past of your forefathers and to have your charters; the past of mine is lost in darkness, and my charters are lost with them. Truthfully we can only date from 1767, when Marc Othmar, who dealt in horses, began to lend money in Agram. It is not a lofty beginning; it is not even a creditable one. But I do not think that to pretend that Marc Othmar, the horse dealer or horse stealer, was a hero and saint would mend matters. I accept him as what he was, but I cannot be proud of him; even sometimes I am on the eve of cursing him; at all events, of wishing he had never existed.'

'My dear Othmar, you are very strange sometimes——'

'Am I? One is never content with what one has. There is nothing strange in that. If you will deign to remember me at all, you will remember that I was never pleased with being the head of the house of Othmar; I would give all its millions for an unblemished descent.'

'Then you are ungrateful to your fortunes, and do not understand your own times.'

'Perhaps I understand them too well, and that is why I despise what they over-estimate.'

'And over-estimate yourself what they have found worth but little. Look at most of our contemporaries and associates. Have their unblemished names served them in much? How many have remembered that *noblesse oblige*? How many of them ally themselves with the mud of the earth for the sake of large dowries? how many mortgage their old lands till they have not a sod left which they can call their own? how many waste all their energies and all their health in a routine of miserable and stupid follies which are hardly even to be dignified as vice?'

She spoke with animation; her cheeks had a faint flush, delicate as that of the waxen bells of the begonia flowers, her eyes were full of light. Othmar looked at her with a passion of regret. If only she had loved him, he thought he could have conquered the world, have renewed the impossibilities of Alexander, have done all that visionary boys dream of doing as they read their Euripides or their Æschylus in a summer noon under blossoming lime trees.

'You will take from Rome what you yourself have carried there,' says a German writer, and it is with love the same thing; you take from it what you carry to it, you get out of it so much spirituality, and no more, than you bear thereto. To others Nadine Napraxine was a coquette, a *mondaine*, a mere *élégante* of the elegant world; but to him she was the one woman of the earth; she could have inspired him with any heroism, she could have moved him to any sacrifice, she could have compensated him for any loss; he saw in her a million possibilities which no one ever saw, which might be only the fruits of his imagination, but yet were wholly real to him, unspeakably lovely and attractive. She had offended him, alienated him, treated his ardour and his earnestness as a baby treats its toys, and his reason condemned her inexorably and often; yet she was the one woman on earth for him, and he had tried to hate her, to drive her out of his memory, and had thought that he succeeded, and had only failed.

'If you were like other men of your generation,' she pursued, 'you would be much more content. You do not care for any of the things which fill up their time. You have magnificent horses, but you never race with them, you never even hunt. You care nothing for cards, or for any games of hazard. You do not shoot except, as you justly observed, a fellow-creature now and then when he provokes you. You do not care to have yourself talked about, which is the supreme felicity of the age you live in; your solitary extravagance is to have operas and concerts given in your own houses with closed doors, like Ludwig of Bavaria, and that seems rather an eccentricity than an extravagance to the world at large. You are a great student, but you care about the contents of your books, not about the binding or the date of their edition, so that you never commit the follies of a bibliophile. You do not care about any of your fine places; you have an idea that you would like a cottage just because you are tired of palaces. You vex women by your indifference to their attractions, and men by your indifference to their pursuits. Because circumstance has made you a conspicuous person with an electric light always upon you, you sigh to be an *homme d'intérieur*, with no light on you at all except that of your own hearth. It is Louis Seize and the locksmith, Domitian and the cabbage-garden, Honorius and the hens, over again. History always repeats itself, and how one wishes that it did not!'

'I am flattered, Madame, that you deign to draw my portrait, since it shows that you have not wholly forgotten my features,' said Othmar, with some bitterness. 'At present I have not discovered the hen, the cabbages, or the keys that will make life worth living to me. No doubt the fault lies with myself.'

'I think you have not the dramatic instinct which alone makes life interesting,' replied Nadine Napraxine. 'You do not divert yourself with the faults, the follies, and the meannesses of men; you sigh over them, and your regret is so poignant that it prevents your seeing how infinitely droll their blunders are in reality.'

'I think,' she continued, 'that there are only two ways of looking on life which make it interesting, or even endurable. The one is the way of Corot, which adores Nature, and can find an absolute ecstasy in the sound of the

- 49 -

wind and the play of the sunshine, and asks nothing more of fate than a mill-stream and a handful of green leaves. The other is the way of Rochefoucauld and of St. Simon, which finds infinite and unending diversion in watching the feebleness and the mistakes of human nature, which regards the world with what I call the dramatic instinct, and amuses itself endlessly with the attitudes and genuflections of its courtiers, the false phrases and the balked calculations. Now, though you are a very clever man, my dear Othmar, you cannot be put in either of these categories. You know too much of the world for the first, and you have too much softness of heart for the second. Now, were you like Baron Fritz———'

'My uncle is the one perfectly happy man that I have ever known,' replied Othmar. 'It is because he is the most perfect of egotists. According to him the sun shines only for the Othmar, as Joshua fancied it only shone for the Israelites.'

'It is not only that,' she said, 'it is because he has the dramatic instinct. He sees the dramatic side to all that he does; suppliant monarchs, bankrupt statesmen, intriguing diplomatists; men who carry him schemes to tunnel the earth from pole to pole, and great ladies who want him to lend them money on their family diamonds; they are all so many comedians in the eyes of Baron Fritz. He pulls their strings and makes them dance at his pleasure. I quite understand how the whole comedy amuses him so greatly that he can never be conscious of a moment of *ennui*. It is a great pity that you are not like that. You would leave such witty memoirs!—for you can be witty,—or you would be if you were not always so melancholy.'

'I regret, Madame,' said Othmar, 'that I cannot alter the manner of my life even to have the honour of amusing you after my death!'

Across the bows of the 'Zostera' at that moment there passed, perilously near, one of the lateen-sailed boats so common on the coast, with their freights of fruits, of fish, of olives, or of market produce. The boat was full of lemons and of oranges, which gleamed like virgin gold in the bright sunshine of the tranquil afternoon. A peasant woman was managing the sail, a young girl was steering.

'What a beautiful face!' said Nadine Napraxine, who had a great love of beauty, and the frank acknowledgment of it of a woman high above all possibilities of envy.

Othmar looked where she pointed.

'A very lovely face,' he said indifferently.

'She does not look like a peasant,' continued Mme. Napraxine; 'that little grey gown speaks of some convent. She steers well, for they were terribly near. Who is that very pretty child, Monsignore? I suppose you know all the flock of which you are given the winter shepherding.'

'Pray do not make me responsible for all the black sheep of these shores,' said Melville, drawing near and looking at the boat, which was going slowly and heavily against the wind, and labouring under a weighty load. He said as he did so, with a little surprise:

'Why, that is Yseulte de Valogne!'

'Yseulte de Valogne! What a name of the Romaunt de la Rose and black-letter Chronicles! Pray who may she be, may I ask?'

'They call her here Cendrillon,' said Melville, a little sadly. 'As for her name, the de Valogne belong to French history; surely you remember to have heard of some of them? Aymar, who fell at the combat of the Thirty; and Adhémar, who was Constable of France under Louis XII.; and Maximin, who was a general under Condé; and Gui, who was ruined by his display at Versailles, a Colonel of the Guard and a great officer of State. The family is as historic as the Louvre itself, but the poor child is literally *sans le sou.*'

'So that she is reduced to sell oranges?' said Nadine. 'How very touching! Othmar will purchase immediately several bales.'

'No, she does not sell oranges,' said Melville, 'but perhaps she is more to be pitied than those who do. A great name and no dower—it is to have silver bells to your shoes but no stockings inside them.'

'Surely she must have stockings, I mean relations?'

'Only very distant ones. She is a far-off cousin of your friend and neighbour the Duchesse de Vannes, who brings her up; that is, sends her to her convent, pays for her frocks, and allows her to pass her holidays at one of de Vannes' country-houses. I do not know that we could reasonably expect the Duchesse to do more, only there are two ways of doing a thing, and she does not do this in the best possible manner.'

'Cri-Cri cannot love a very pretty girl of sixteen, it would not be in nature, certainly not in her nature,' said the Princess, with one of her moments of frankness. 'I imagine they will make her embrace the religious life; what else can they do with her?'

'It is what they will probably end with,' said Melville, with a tinge of sadness. 'It is hard for a girl of noble blood and no dower to end otherwise in France. The men who ought to marry her, her equals, will marry instead some Americans with dollars, whose fathers were stokers or pork-butchers.'

'But are there no other de Valogne?'

'None; she is the last of a family which was as extravagant as it was distinguished. Othmar may have heard of her father, the last Comte de Valogne; he was a *viveur enragé*, and finished the little that had been left by Count Gui, the hero of Versailles, and the fortune of his wife as well, who was a De Creusac. She died in childbed. Her mother had the care of the child, and he went on with his life of pleasure until he broke his neck riding at La Marche. The old Marquise de Creusac, when she also died, could not leave her granddaughter a farthing. The de Creusac had been ruined in the Revolution, and the sons of the Marquise, who would never have anything to do with their brother-in-law, were both killed in the war of '70. There was no one left but the Duchesse de Vannes, who was a third cousin of de Valogne, to do anything. She took the child in her charge, as I have said, and has behaved admirably, in the letter of charity, if something has been lacking of the spirit. So long as the girl is being educated the thing is easy; but when the time comes when she must leave her convent, as she will have to do in two years' time, the problem will not be so easy of solution; they will have to decide on her future; at present her fate has been easily settled, but soon the terrible question will arise,—who will marry her without a dower? I believe they mean to make her enter the religious life, as you said; for the men who probably would marry her for sake of alliance with the de Vannes, will be those with whom the de Vannes would utterly refuse to ally themselves.'

'A convent! Good heavens, for a child like a Greuze picture!' exclaimed Othmar.

Melville added sadly:

'It is a refuge; but myself, I would never have the religious life embraced only for its safety. I never approve of looking at Deity as a superior sort of chaperon. If all the soul be not aspirant of its own accord to a spiritual sacrifice the vows are a mere shibboleth.'

'What soul shrined in a healthy body would aspire to the cloister at sixteen?' thought Othmar, as the Princess said, 'All this is very interesting, Monsignore, but it does not explain how a *protégée* of my neighbours, the high and mighty de Vannes, comes to be rowing in a boat full of oranges.'

'Ah, that I cannot tell you,' said Melville, 'but I believe her foster-mother has a *bastide* near Nice; it may be she is with her foster-mother now. I knew her well when she was a little child, living with the old Marquise de Creusac in that extreme but refined and reserved poverty of which only the old noblesse has the secret. The Marquise was one of the sweetest and most pious women I have ever had the honour to know; but she could, if necessary, have withered a king into the earth with a glance. The child promised to be like her, but had something *bouillante* and impetuous, which had come to her from her father, and which, beneath her high-bred manner and her chastened tone, made her, as a baby, intensely interesting.'

'Dear Monsignore,' said the Princess, with a little impatience, 'surely you have mistaken your vocation, and should have been a writer of novels; you draw portraits with the skill of Octave Feuillet.'

'I have only said what I have seen,' said Melville, good-humouredly. 'Probably Feuillet only does the same.'

The boat with the oranges had passed ahead towards the shore, its Venetian red side was dipping in the trough of the waves, its old striped sail was swaying in the wind; there was a speck of gold in the sun where the oranges were.

'You had better rescue this distressed damsel and marry her, Othmar!' said the Princess Napraxine, with an unkind little laugh. 'She seems made on purpose for you. She has the unsullied descent which you are always sighing for, and you certainly can dispense with a *dot*.'

For answer he only looked at her; but she understood his answer.

Melville vaguely understood also that in his innocent praises of his Cinderella he had unwittingly struck a false chord, and he was too much a man of the world not to be grieved at his involuntary failure in tact. The boat meanwhile was fast growing to a mere speck of red and yellow colour, soon to be wholly lost in the blue radiance of sea and sky.

'You have at times bought some Greuzes, if I remember,' continued the Princess. 'They are pretty, soft, conventional, but I do not know that your gallery is much the richer for them.'

'They belong to another time than ours,' said Othmar. 'I imagine Talleyrand was right when he said that no one born since '89 can know how sweet human life can become.'

'And how elegant human manners can be,' added Melville. 'Cendrillon has something of that old grace; when she was two years old she curtseyed as though she were Sevigné's self.'

'What a paragon!' said Madame Napraxine. 'Poverty and all the Graces! An irresistible combination. The time I should have liked to live in would have been Louis Treize's; what perfect costume, what picturesque wars, what admirable architecture! Is this child at Sacré Cœur, did you say, Monsignore?'

'That would be too extravagant for her place as Cendrillon,' replied Melville. 'No; I think they were wise not to put her amidst all those great ladies in embryo; she has been educated by the Dames de Ste. Anne, at a remote village called Faiël in the Morbihan. She has had a pale girlhood there, like the arum-lily that blossoms under the moss-grown oaks.'

'How poetic you are!' said the Princess Napraxine, with a smile which brought a flush of embarrassment even to the world-bronzed cheek of Melville. 'Men are so much more romantic than women. Here are Clotilde de Vannes and I, who only see that, as this young girl has no dower, the very best place for her in the world is a convent, melancholy but inevitable; whereas you and Othmar, merely because she has pretty hair which the sun shines on as she goes past amongst her oranges, are already thinking that some one ought to rise out of the sea to marry her, with a duke's *couronne* in one hand and a veil of old d'Alençon lace in the other! Certainly those things do happen. If she were an impudent *écuyère* at Hengler's, or a Californian who never had a grandfather, the duke's *couronne* would no doubt appear on her horizon. By the way, pending her eternal retreat, does Cri-Cri allow her to be seen at all?'

'You will probably see her at Millo. I saw her there last week, and made her cry by reminding her of her babyhood on the isle; and of her grandmother, whom she adored. She is with the Duchesse now, because there is typhus fever at the convent, and the pupils are all dispersed; but Millo is scarcely a congenial air for a poor relation, who is also a proud one.'

'Ah! she is a good advertisement of Cri-Cri's virtues, *elle en a besoin*,' said the Princess Napraxine, with her merciless little laugh. 'And de Vannes, what does he say to so pretty a relative?'

'A man like de Vannes never sees that a young girl of that type exists.'

'Hum—m—mph!' she murmured dubiously. 'That depends on a great many circumstances. Propinquity and *ennui* will make Ste. Scholastique herself sought like the Krauss or Jeanne Granier. Millo is certainly a very odd kind of home for your woodland arum-lily. If she have any intelligence at all, and relate what she sees when she gets back to Faiël, the good Dames de Ste. Anne will have the monastic enjoyment of scandal gratified to the uttermost.'

'I believe she lives entirely in the schoolroom whilst at Millo,' said Melville, a little impatiently. He wished he had never spoken the name of Yseulte de Valogne, the name which seemed to belong to *le temps quand la Reine Berthe fila*. He had one of those instincts of having spoken unwisely, one of those presentiments of impending disaster, which come to finely organised and much-experienced minds, and are called by blunter and slower brains mere nervous nonsense.

When the other day the tall factory chimney fell at Bradford, the birds which built in it had flown away before the workmen—stupidly eating their breakfasts till the bricks tumbled about their ears—had looked up and seen any danger.

---

# CHAPTER V.

As Othmar leaned against the side of the yacht and let his eyes dwell on her face, unseen by him so long, his regard let something of the emotion which he felt escape him, and betrayed that the chill indifference with which he had met her again had been but the mere mask of pride, though it might be a mask which he would be strong enough always to wear in her presence.

'Yonder is S. Pharamond,' he said, conscious of his momentary loss of self-control, as he pointed to some round towers which rose above woods of ilex trees and magnolias. 'If you would allow them to land me there instead of at Nice I should be grateful, and perhaps you would honour me with landing too: the house is somewhat neglected, as I have been away so long; but they will be at least able to give you a cup of tea.'

'With pleasure, if Wilkes likes it,' said the Princess, as she joined her friend. 'I never knew you had a place upon this coast; surely you never named it when—when I knew you first?'

'Most likely not,' said Othmar, 'I have been seldom there. It was a favourite house of my father's in his rare moments of leisure, but I have never cared for the air or for the world of Nice. I have lent it sometimes to my friends.'

'What do you not lend to your friends? In that respect you have made yourself honey, and the flies have eaten you without hesitation.'

'If the honey be not in the hive it ought to be eaten. There is a landing-place in my grounds, and the house is not more than a quarter of a mile distant, if such a distance do not alarm you. I know that you are no great pedestrian, Princess.'

'Why should one be when there are so many more agreeable modes of progression? *On ne doit jamais se punir pour rien.*'

'I have walked twenty miles for my own pleasure very often,' said Lady Brancepeth, who approached them.

'Oh, but you are English; we were just saying that all English people are like beavers, you must be sawing and drilling and building and dragging something or other all through the length of your days. I could walk, I think I could walk right across Russia, if there were any wise object to be obtained by it, but simply to walk, as a mad dog runs, from a sort of blind impulsion!—no, that is beyond me.'

'You are such a curious union, Nadine, of languor and energy, of indifference and of potentialities,' began her friend.

'My energy is latent,' she said, interrupting her. 'I do not waste it on every-day trifles, as you waste yours. You always use forty-horse power to boil an egg or make a box of wax matches. That is an English idea of energy.'

'Your grandmother, the Princesse d'Yssingeaux, was English by birth.'

'So was Othmar's mother. That is why he and I have something of the beaver in us, but calmed, controlled, kept in reserve; we do not waste our time and timber damming up threads of water, but we shall be ready if an inundation occur.'

'Othmar, perhaps,' said Lady Brancepeth.

'I have a great deal more energy than he,' said Nadine Napraxine, with a smile, as she leaned back in the wicker lounging-chair, looking as indolent as a Turkish woman, and as delicate and useless as a painted butterfly.

The schooner in twenty minutes' time landed them at a creek, with a little marble quay, shadowed by great pines and eucalyptus trees; there was a pavilion on the small pier, a pretty kiosque all white and blue and gold, with twisted pillars and Moorish arabesques.

'Remember, nothing here is of my taste or choice,' said Othmar; 'I have not been at the place for ten years. Would you like to rest? They can bring your tea to you; or would you come up to the house at once?'

'*Va pour le château*,' said Nadine Napraxine; 'I never care for the preface of a story.'

'I fear you will find it a dull story,' said he, as they left the quay and passed up a steep path, always under the shadow of the trees.

'What a misfortune for him that he inherited so much! It prevents him enjoying any thing,' she said to Melville; who replied, a little drily:

'I do not think it is what he inherited which prevents his enjoyment, Princess; it is more probably what he encountered and sighed for vainly. Life holds many of these ironies.'

'If I were he,' she continued, ignoring the reply, 'I should care for nothing but that power which he, in common with other great capitalists, possesses. To be able to make a war possible or impossible by the mere inclining of your wand of gold—that must be the most interesting of all possible kinds of influence.'

'Yes, the financier is the modern Merlin, but then there is Vivien——'

'In Mr. Tennyson's poem, not out of it,' said Princess Nadine, sceptically; but she knew very well that Vivien was then walking under the shade of her own great red parasol, with its group of humming-birds embroidered on its left side.

The pathway ascended steeply through the woods, bordered with datura and geranium, which were still blossoming gaily; here and there was a wooden bench, a majolica seat, a little statue; the ground was of shining shingle; it had been kept in perfect order, awaiting its owner, for ten years. After about a quarter of a mile it ended on a level space of the red rock up which it had climbed. Here had been laid out a fairy-like and fantastic garden, lawns, palms, fountains, walls of shrubs, and groves of camellias and azaleas, spreading before a château, which was, in architecture, a miniature Maintenon, and in position stood high enough to look over the sea in front of it.

'What a delicious place!' said Nadine; 'and in a month or two, when all those azaleas flower—if I had known you had owned such a bijou, I would have told you to lend it to us. It makes La Jacquemerille a mere trumpery toy.'

'I would lend you nothing,' said Othmar, in her ear; 'I would have given you everything—once.'

Then he added aloud, 'This is somewhat trumpery also, I fear; modern things are so apt to have that look. They are like the *articles de Paris*, which cost enormously, but are only plush and ormolu after all. However, Viollet le Duc built this house; so it may be a little better than its neighbours. Only I should like statelier and simpler gardens myself; I should like high box hedges and old-fashioned plants. But I suppose they would not go with the Mediterranean.'

'You like anything simple and homely; you will have to marry Margot, or Phœbe, or Grethel, off a farm,' said the Princess, with some contempt. She was a hothouse flower herself, and despised thyme and dog-roses.

'I might do worse,' said Othmar, as he ushered them into the house, which contained some wonderful china, some admirable modern pictures, some fine statuary, and more French luxury than its master cared to have surround him.

'It is exquisite,' said the Princess, after wandering through it, and returning to a room opening on the gardens; a room hung with tawny plush, embroidered with white roses and blue irises. The chairs and couches matched the walls, a gilt cornice ran round the oval ceiling, which was painted *in tempera* with the story of Undine. 'How many more houses have you, Othmar, standing like so many open empty caskets waiting for you to put the jewel of life into them? Really, how many have you? Come, tell me!'

'I have too many,' said Othmar. 'But excess always carries its own retribution; amongst them all I have no home; none that I feel home-like. I can imagine what it is—a *chez soi* that one cares about and desires to return to—but I do not possess it.'

'Make it,' said Melville; 'that is always in the power of every man who is not a priest.'

'I suppose it is,' said Othmar. 'But it has never seemed very easy to me. The fire of the hearth is like the coal from the altar: it comes from heaven, and can scarcely be commanded.'

He glanced as he spoke at Nadine Napraxine, who was lying back against the golden gleams of the plush of her couch; she had a tea-rose in her hand which she had plucked from the gardens. She looked dream-like and ethereal. She had on her lips that little smile which meant so much and yet said nothing, and was half compassion and half disdain, and partially, also, amusement. If she had been mistress here and in all his other houses, he thought, each one of them would have been Eden to him. But that had not been Melville's meaning.

At that moment his servants brought in the tea noiselessly and quickly: little Saxe cups, frosted cakes, forced strawberries, appearing on great old plateaux of gold,—as though he had been served there every day instead of having been absent ten years.

'Really, Othmar, you have a little of the Haroun Alraschid, though you do not care for your throne,' said Melville: 'who would have imagined that returning from Asia last night you would have tea all ready made for your friends?'

'My friends reconcile me to my house,' said Othmar; 'you will leave almost a perfume of home behind you, these rooms will seem lonely no more.'

'The rooms are quite perfect,' said Princess Nadine, 'but still I think we will have our tea out of doors; the sun is still brilliant. We have now and then little fits of rurality; when we have those we sit on a terrace and take tea; that is as near rusticity as we care to go.'

She walked through one of the doorways into the air as she spoke.

To Othmar the golden-coloured room with its white roses and blue irises seemed to grow dark as she left it.

As she passed out to the gardens his people brought him a note; it was inside a silver-grey envelope, with a silver *couronne* upon it, and on a silver-grey card was written a very pressingly worded invitation to dinner the following night with his neighbours the Duc and Duchesse de Vannes.

They had just heard of his arrival; they would have a few people; they begged him not to be formal, &c. &c. The château nearest to him was Millo, their favourite winter retreat; a gorgeous and fantastic place, with many a gilded cupola and shining dome which caught the sunshine from the sea, amidst groves of magnolia and woods of ilex. He had not been to Millo for ten years. When he had been last there the Duc had been just married to a famous beauty, and he had known them very well in Paris ever since that time. They were not people for whom he cared much: Alain de Vannes was a sporting man, and his wife was one of the leaders of fashion, with half a hundred lovers given to her, rightly or wrongly, by report. They were, however, legitimist in politics to the backbone. Neither of their families had ever pandered to Emperor or Elysée, and they were, despite their easy morals and their profound indifference to each other, exceedingly exclusive, and, with all their nonchalance, even arrogant.

'It must be a strange house for that poor little girl,' he thought as he threw the card aside, and remembered the Greuze face in the Venetian red boat. Millo was not more than a mile off him, at one point their woods and his joined, and looking from his terrace any day he could see the gilded minarets and the varicoloured tiles of their villas shining in the light against billows of dark evergreen foliage.

'How soon they know you are here!' said Nadine Napraxine, as he spoke of the invitation to her. 'You will go, of course; you cannot have any engagements?'

'Will you be there?'

'I do not know; yes, perhaps. I never make up my mind until the last hour. People say it is cruel when they have dinners; it leaves a place blank; but how can you be sure what you wish to do until the moment comes? I detest dinners. When we have really become civilised we shall each of us eat in solitude, or, at the least, each behind his own screen. Why should one of the unloveliest of the operations of nature be performed in public? The flowers, and the plate, and the footmen cannot really embellish it; indeed, they only make it the more grotesque.'

'How droll you are, Nadine!' said Lady Brancepeth. 'You have certainly a monopoly of singular ideas.'

'I wish my ideas were general,' answered the Princess. 'When the world has really refined itself it will look on our eating in society as we look now on savages eating with their fingers. Some of our friends cannot even have a little love affair but they must go and eat prawns, and quails, and *petits fours* together in a café; and if a hero comes home from a war anywhere his countrymen at once make him eat and drink in public by way of showing their respect for him. The whole thing is absurd. The only creature that is not offensive when it eats is a bird. Just one little dive in a rose, or under a vine-leaf, and it has breakfasted. But we!——'

'When a very pretty woman eats a strawberry, the bird is not very much her superior,' murmured Melville.

'Reverend father,' said the Princess, 'you have no business to know whether one is pretty or not. Fruit, perhaps, does keep something of the golden age about it; but our dinners!—were I a man I would never see the woman I admired taking her share of diseased livers, tortured fish, slaughtered songsters. They are fond of writing nowadays about a higher humanity which will succeed to ours; but my idea of it would be that it should be fed like Fénelon's islanders by only breathing sweet odours. That would be even better than the bird's dip in the rose.'

'Then you will not go to Millo?' persisted Othmar.

'Who knows what one may do in twenty-four hours?'

The servants had carried the gold trays out into the garden after her. Melville and Lady Brancepeth, who were more comfortable in the embrace of their plush couches, returned within-doors; Othmar drew his chair nearer to hers, and offered her a cigarette.

'Rurality always wants this consolation, Princess,' he said, as he did so.

'Thanks; not till I have finished my strawberries. They are delicious. How do you manage your households? If we go home unexpectedly anywhere we always find the servants away, the major-domo drunk, the house topsy-turvy, and not a thing to eat within twenty miles. How did you keep them at this point of perfection?'

'They are never sure that I may not arrive at any moment. If servants be not ready at any hour of the day or night they are not worth their salt. Then I have very faithful stewards——'

'One marvel does not explain another. The fidelity is perhaps more astonishing than the perpetual readiness.'

'I reward fidelity; most people limit themselves to accepting it. If you do not pay your servant well he will help himself.'

'I am sure we pay—pay endlessly. Platon spends Heaven knows what on the servants, but he gets only a mob of rogues, who rob him right and left.'

'I have no right to suppose the Prince less wise than myself; but perhaps there is other payment as well as money in which he does not deal. I let the humblest man in my service have plenty of hope; there is no moral tonic so bracing; each of them knows that he may rise if he only deserve it. Then, again, I am heedful to have my house-stewards men of high character; a house-steward is one's viceroy—one cannot be too careful in choosing him.'

'I should never have supposed you cared about those things, Othmar,' she said, in much surprise, as she stared at him, a strawberry held uneaten against her lips.

'One must think about them or be at war with one's conscience,' he answered. 'That is the tedium of life; its duties are so inexorable and so wearisome.'

'Is an easy conscience absolutely necessary to you?'

'No; I could easily imagine circumstances under which a guilty one would make me carry it lightly.'

A gleam of the old passionate emotion which she had once known in him passed for a moment into his eyes with gloom and fire mingled. He repressed it; he did not wish her to believe that she had still the power over his life which she actually possessed. He heard her voice saying always, 'I will have no melodramatic passions to disturb me; they are absurd, they are out of date, they are tiresome.'

And she had said it out of no virtue, only out of sheer shallowness and indifference.

'That is a very shocking sentiment,' she said demurely now, as she ate another strawberry. 'At least, one is bound to say so; Monsignore in there would certainly say so. Indeed, from Monsignore's point of view, one would certainly think it so; but as all we modern people, whatever church we ostensibly belong to, are all so completely of one mind that we know we are only automata, made up of nerve-centres and different gases, I do not see why we should necessarily have consciences at all, do you? Why should we have one any more than the zostera from which I named that yacht?'

'Only because the zosteræ have no traditions of a conscience, all men have.'

'All men? Savages have not, primitive races have not; and how should we know whether the zostera has or has not? She may have a very perfect system of ethics, sitting on her rocks in reach of the tide—I should think, indeed, she had a sort of Buddhism.'

'You named that yacht?' he said abruptly.

'Yes; Geraldine had her built last year. He is not like you; he has not a superstition that one is bound to go on sailing in the same ship all one's life, however old-fashioned she may grow.'

'Lord Geraldine has many superiorities over me. He has the patience to play at Platonic cicisbeism as children play for counters,' said Othmar, with a brusque contempt.

'That is neither a well-bred speech nor a true one,' said Nadine Napraxine very calmly, as she set down her cup.

'Its breeding I cannot defend, its truth I do,' he answered coldly. 'There are men who can spend their lives carrying a woman's fan, and ask for nothing more at her hands; they have merits, no doubt, but they are not those which I appreciate.'

'Poor Ralph! if he heard you!' she said, with a little yawn which she could not control, though she tried to stifle it with a cigarette. 'He thinks himself far more manly than you because he shoots fur and feather, and you do not kill anything—except a man now and then!'

'I may yet add to the list of the latter,' said Othmar.

'The Mongolians have made you very savage,' she said, as she lighted the cigarette. 'And you used to be so gentle.'

'I used to be many things that I have ceased to be since the twentieth of April a year and eight months ago,' said Othmar.

She had forgotten the date which he remembered so accurately, the date of the day on which they had parted in her own room in Paris, with the smell of the lilac of the avenue coming in through the open windows, and the sunset rays, as they came through the rose-coloured blinds, touching her fair face, and the curl of her long dark lashes, and the beautiful mouth with the little cruel languid smile on it as she had said, 'I will have no melodramatic passions to disturb me.'

She looked at him now with the demure un-selfconsciousness of a child.

'Ah! I never could remember dates,' she murmured. 'I was the despair of all my governesses, I had such a bad memory.'

'It is convenient sometimes,' said Othmar, a little bitterly. Why were all those past hours written on his remembrance as the chisel writes on stone, whilst she had shaken off their memories as a bird shakes a summer rain off its wings?

'And how,' he added with an effort, 'with such a defective brain as you describe, have you become one of the most cultured women of Europe? Does forgetfulness of—dates—enhance the power of acquiring other knowledge?'

'I think it leaves the brain freer,' she answered, in that serene way which she had with her when she was intending that a man should never forget her whatever she might choose to forget.

'No doubt,' he said impatiently. 'No doubt learned women have never been very tender ones.'

'Learned! what a terrific word. Would you call a mere poor frivolous *mondaine* like me by the same word that described Lady Jane Grey and Mrs. Somerville? I know a few languages; I had *bonnes* of every nation when I was a baby; and I have read Schopenhauer and Herbert Spencer, and I assure you that one bored me as much as the other. But learned! would a *bas bleu* eat your strawberries or smoke your cigarettes?'

'Or take all my heart and my soul out of me?' he thought, as he answered, 'No; certainly your one great science, Madame, was never learned either in the nursery, or out of Schopenhauer and Herbert Spencer. It is the perfection of high art; and you, like all supreme artists, cannot pause to remember what your studies may cost to your subjects.'

She did not ask him what art or science he meant; she lighted a second cigarette and said, in her sweetest voice, 'I do not think you are quite so even-tempered as you used to be, Count Othmar. Look, the sun is low; it is time to be going homeward. What are Monsignore and Evelyn doing? Will you call them, please?'

'Stay yet a little while; I have not seen you for so long,' he murmured, ashamed and irritated at his own weakness in letting the words escape him.

'Naturally you have not,' she said, with a gay laugh, 'since you have been in Asia and I in Europe. Why did you go to Asia? People do not do that sort of thing nowadays. If they be annoyed they walk down to their club and play hard, or they ride a horse at a steeplechase, and in a week they think no more about it. And why did you have that duel with de Sénélac? It was very imprudent. I had told you I could not bear that kind of melodrama. Nobody knew certainly, but that was only because they were all stupid; any one might have known. And Sénélac never left his bed for six months; and have you heard that he will limp, they say, for ever?'

Othmar, with a gesture, intimated that the misfortune of his late adversary was a matter of utter indifference.

'If you be sorry that he limps,' he said impatiently, 'be sorry that you gave him your bouquet to carry. Princess, you are very fond of psychological studies, but you do not like to be reminded of what others pay for them. You know well enough what men suffer for you, and through you, but you do not choose ever to blame yourself for making them do so. The world has not changed; the mode of expression may have altered, but men feel as they felt in the days of David or of Æschylus. Love is what it was then, a mere passing pleasure or pain to many, but to some the herald of heaven or of hell, the begetter of heroism or of crime.'

'My dear Othmar, pray excuse me,' said Nadine Napraxine, 'you talk beautifully, you always did, but I cannot stay to hear you when the sun is just going down, and we have only a yacht that crawls to take us home to dinner. It is my fault that it crawls: he would have had a steam one if I had not prevented him. I detest smoke and machinery, but still certainly without them one crawls. Monsignore, will you come if you have finished talking about the Little Sisters of the Poor?'

Othmar's face grew cold, a sombre displeasure darkened his eyes, he drew back and let Melville join Madame Napraxine. He himself walked beside her friend down the path through the woods talking, but not sensible of what he said, watching the red sunshade with its embroidered humming-birds pass before him under the boughs.

As they neared the quay he took from the hands of one of his men two bouquets of gardenias and orchids, and offered them to the two ladies; they were in pretty cornucopiæ of silvered wicker-work. Any one would have thought that there had been the preparation of a week for this afternoon visit.

'You are *bon prince*,' said Madame Napraxine as she took her orchids, 'why will you pretend to be a barbarian? The little graceful amenities of the world become you, and you do them so well, though you do them so seldom; why will you make yourself *un homme de foyer—manqué*? It is much nicer,' she added in a low murmur, 'to give me a bouquet than to shoot another man for carrying one.'

He did not answer. Her jests jarred on him.

When they reached the quay the sun was setting, the boat was waiting, the sailors immovable, their oars held straight in the air.

'Adieu, Othmar!' said the Princess Nadine gaily. 'Your château is marvellous, your orchids are exquisite, and your tea was enchanting; we will leave you all alone in your poetic solitude, and when you want prose and society you will come to La Jacquemerille.'

'Will you not honour me again?' he said, angry at his own weakness. 'Would you not dine with me to-morrow night? Or the day after to-morrow? I think the Prince would come.'

'Oh! Platon would come certainly,' said Nadine Napraxine, with a smile; 'you are his especial friend. He shall come to you alone; then you can talk to him as much as you like about the burning of Moscow and—and—all those other dates for which you have so admirable a memory!'

She would say no more than that, and her musical slight laugh tantalised his ear as the boat was pushed off in the deep blue water, and the seamen bent above their oars.

Otho Othmar leaned against the marble balustrade and watched them row away towards the schooner, with an anger in which vain regrets and baffled desires were mingled disconsolately. He remained there till the sun was gone down, and the white canvas of the yacht had passed out of sight round a bend of the shore.

When he retraced his steps to his solitary house, he saw a tea-rose lying beside the gilded garden chair which she had occupied as she ate her strawberries. It was the one which she had gathered and dropped. He picked it up and put it in his coat.

'*Quand on aime on n'a que vingt ans*,' he thought with scorn for himself.

He entered the golden drawing-room, wrote a formal note of invitation to the Prince and Princess Napraxine, and said to one of his servants, 'Send a messenger over with this letter the first thing in the morning to the villa that is called La Jacquemerille.' Yet he had come from Asia with the firm resolve to show the Princess Napraxine that he had conquered all passion for her; and he was not on the whole a weak man.

# CHAPTER VI.

He dined alone; a few telegrams would have filled his rooms, but he did not care for society, which he thought only came to him because he was one of the few owners of milliards in Europe. He sat alone after dinner in the salon which she had admired, with the light of half a hundred wax candles bringing out the golden gleams in the plush, the colours of the embroidered irises, the dead gold of the cornice and panels, while a fire of olive wood glowed under the carvings of the mantelpiece of porphyry. The plush curtains, with the lace beneath them, veiled the shuttered windows; outside the night was calm, there was no sound anywhere. The words of Melville came back to him as he sat there in the midst of the luxury and of the loneliness: 'To make a home is in the power of any man who is not a priest.'

It did not seem to him to lie in his. He could have bought a principality, but he could not buy a home. Love alone could create that, and the only woman he had loved for years was Nadine Napraxine.

If she had been what he wished to him, would she have made him this ideal home—she, capricious, indifferent, disdainful, *mondaine*, as she had said, in every habit, thought, and attitude of her life? Perhaps not; probably not, he knew; yet she alone would have had power to make a melody out of the discords of his desires and his discontent; she alone seemed to him to fill the vacant places, to smile across the solitary room, to have left the lingering perfume of her presence there, as the orange flowers left their fragrance in the cabinet in which they were laid for a moment.

Otho Othmar was one of the richest men in Europe; he was often disposed to regret it, as many persons regret that to which they have been born. He did not think it a thing to be vain of; he was even occasionally ashamed of it. It seemed to him that when you were so much richer than most of your fellows you were required to be very much better than they; and it is not always agreeable, nor often easy, to be so. When he signed 'Othmar' it was as when an emperor signs his name, and with a stroke of the pen he could give away millions with as much ease as lesser mortals can scatter pence. This facility was no pleasure to him. Though he was well aware that riches are the one ruling power of the modern world, and comprise in themselves the wishing cap and the magician's wand, Excalibur and Holy Grail, he did not greatly prize his possession of them; perhaps because they had been always before him and about him in profusion from his birth.

The Othmar fortune had been steadily growing for a century and a half. At the commencement Marc Othmar, a Croat, native of Agram, had been a poor man enough—a horse dealer, some said a horse stealer—what precisely never was known. Agram is not a very greatly frequented place, and records get easily mildewed and dim in it. Whether he began life as pedlar, or peasant, or, as some affirmed, as a robber of wild colts, Marc Othmar at forty years old was a money-lender, commission agent, and banker, and at sixty had become a millionaire, known of far beyond Croatia, and had laid the foundations of one of the great financial houses of Eastern Europe.

His son quadrupled his possessions and extended his operations westward and northward. His grandson fell upon the hard times of the Napoleonic wars as on a bed of roses; and from the misfortunes of Austria and Prussia, and the necessities of Pitt's England, made gold as rapidly as though he had had the philosopher's stone in a crucible. He grew into a very colossus of riches, and his houses did their business in Vienna, Paris, London, and Frankfort. He married the daughter of a French duke, and made his central house of business in Paris.

His eldest son Stefan, who inherited all his astuteness, succeeded him in due course in the direction of affairs, ably seconded by his brother Friederich, and in his turn married the daughter of an English nobleman, by whom he had one son, Otho, who was chiefly educated in England, and who had little or nothing of the Othmar type in feature or in character.

He was a boy of infinite promise, and of no ordinary mind, but, despite his personal and intellectual gifts, he was a bitter disappointment to his father; and the indifference, which at times deepened into contempt, with which the lad reviewed the origin and the employment of the fortunes of his house seemed to him nothing short of blasphemy. Stefan Othmar himself was a man of excessive arrogance, but it was a bourgeois arrogance, proud of its own sources and dominion, and capable of infinite self-abasement in the pursuit of self-interest. That his boy should revolt against his descent and despise the future before him was a fact so hideous and so amazing in his sight that, had he not known his dead wife to have been the purest and coldest of women, he would almost have doubted that his own blood ran in the veins of his degenerate heir.

As Otho grew towards manhood the distance between them widened more and more. That a fastidious fine gentleman, a fantastic and futile dreamer, a mere visionary and dilettante, should be the outcome of a hundred and fifty years of financial success and ambition seemed to Count Stefan so frightful a mockery of fortune, that he cursed his own folly in having wedded a patrician, instead of some woman of a common but ambitious stock who would have given him successors content, and solely content, with the superb position of princes of finance, and capable of doubling and quadrupling those many millions which were his own ecstasy. The very virtues of his son alarmed him as hardly any vices would have done. The youth was so delicate of mind and taste, so devout and chaste of habit, so meditative and so solitary by choice, that his father grew alarmed lest he should actually do what he at times threatened, and consecrate himself to the Catholic priesthood. He took a violent remedy.

He went to one of the most seductive and most venal women of the day, and said to her, 'Win this boy from his dreams or he will become a monk.'

She undertook the mission, and succeeded in it. She destroyed all that was spiritual and innocent in him with the merciless witchery of the courtesan, which is like the tide of burning lava: no grass will spring where the scoria has spread. He awoke in her arms without a faith. He never again dreamed of the religious life. She earned well the estate in Franche-Comté and the large sum in rouleaux which his father settled on her; but nothing in after-life could ever give him back those heavenward aspirations, that purity of soul, which she had swept away as with a wave of fire. Like the young Reichstadt before him, he had wasted all the splendour and innocence of a first passion on a wanton who had betrayed him for gold. The first passion of a boy colours all his future; the bitter-sweet flavour of this remained with him through all his later years. Love without it was tasteless; love with it was worthless. He said once to his father: 'You had better have killed me than have given me to Sara Vernon.'

'Who passes by the gates of disillusion has died twice.' His father had pushed him with a hard hand through those gates, believing that they led to the path of self-knowledge and of empire over men. Stefan Othmar had not wanted a poet, a scholar, a philanthropist, or a priest for his successor; he had wanted a cold-hearted, clear-headed, unscrupulous, unyielding financier to hold, and even to increase, the mighty powers and possessions of which the name of Othmar was a symbol to the world.

But the crime he had committed did not obtain for him what he desired. The merciless cynicism with which he had destroyed the faith and the purity of his son did not ensure its object. The youth remained as aloof in mind from the traditions of his house, and as disdainful in spirit of them, as he had been before. He consented, indeed, with apathy, to put his signature to the deeds which made him one of the chiefs of the house, but that was all which Stefan Othmar gained by his son's immeasurable loss. Some four years later, when Otho was two-and-twenty years of age, Stefan Othmar died suddenly on the steps of his great hotel in the Boulevard St. Germain, as he was ascending them after an audience at the Tuileries, in which he had been the master of the situation, and Napoléon Trois the suppliant. He died of fulminant apoplexy without an instant's warning; but his affairs were left in the most perfect order. His brother Fritz remained, who had been his *alter ego* all his life, and nothing was altered in the House of Othmar, of which his son became supreme master.

The young man received the news far away in the forest recesses of Lahore, at the court of an Indian prince, where he was being feasted with royal honours in the course of his travels over the world. There had been no sympathy between his father and himself; their temperaments had been as opposite as the poles; little sentiment of personal affection mingled with his sudden consciousness that he was absolute lord of his own destinies. His first impulse was to use the power into which he had entered to destroy, at a blow, all that his forefathers had been a century and a half in building up for him. 'It is a mass of corruption; it shall perish,' he said to himself, with the ruthless integrity, the unsparing fanaticism, of a generous and high-souled youth. But when he returned to England and came face to face with all his responsibilities and powers, he found that which he had thought so easy was quite impossible to accomplish as he desired to accomplish it. His first impulse was to throw the whole into liquidation and efface the House of Othmar from financial existence for ever. But to do so was but a dream; the financial world would not have released him from his obligations; his only living relative, his father's brother and partner, Baron Friederich Othmar, stoutly refused to suffer that to be done which would, in his sight, have been a greater crime than many murders.

Against his desires and against his conscience, he had, on reaching his majority, been half persuaded, half coerced, by his father to associate himself in legal form with the house. The act had been one of filial sacrifice, and it hung like a wallet of stones about his neck. He found that his power had its limits; that he could no more disengage himself from all the operations and engagements of his firm than a young king can emancipate himself from the trammels of court and constitution. He had a right to ruin himself, but he had no right to ruin all those whose fortunes were interwoven with the enterprises of his predecessors. Irritated and disappointed he resigned himself to the inevitable, and remained the 'master of milliards,' with as much regret as the young Francis Joseph accepted the diadem of Austria. The cloth of gold in which they, his forefathers, had wrapped him remained upon him, and sometimes he thought it a very shirt of Nessus.

Sometimes he was almost tempted to take the vow of poverty for the sake of getting rid of it, but he was restrained by two recollections—one that he had no spiritual faith, the other that mankind in general would have voted him insane. A profound melancholy, without any definite or special cause, grew upon him; he felt the sense of an immense responsibility, which he saw no manner of using with proportionate usefulness. The sophism that duties unsought may be disregarded did not satisfy his conscience, whilst his knowledge of the world told him that to do harm is as easy as to kiss your hand, whilst to effect any great good is as hard as to move the mountains from their bases. Public charity only fills the pockets of greedy speculators; private charity too often raises up a festering mass of imposture. The rich man goes through the world as a sheep through briars in spring time. If he be a perfect egotist, he is happy enough; if he have thought and feeling, he is depressed by the universal greed around him, and by the absolute impotence of all religions to bridle it.

Otho Othmar remained always sensible of a bitter irritation and degradation whenever he recalled the sources of the wealth he enjoyed: the ruin of prosperous countries, the wholesale slaughter of wars, the distress or disgrace of ancient nobilities, the impoverishment of nations. True, there was another side to the throne of Plutus, on which his fathers had seated themselves; by their means, no doubt, enterprises had been carried out for which humanity, on the whole, was materially, if not spiritually, the better. Canals, deserts, mines, cities, colonies, ocean ways, had felt the vivifying powers of the great Othmar loans; but the evil appeared to him far to out-balance the good, and all the wealth seemed to him tainted. He had considerable pride, in a shape with which men would not have sympathised. He fancied that the inherited nobility of his French and English blood was always at war with the blood of the Croat bankers by whom he had been begotten. Though his position was one which almost all the world envied, it was one which galled himself. Titles had been offered him, but he had contemptuously rejected them. He was Othmar; the name spoke to all the ears of Europe; he did not consider that the story it told could be either changed or buried by smothering it underneath the blaze of some princeship or dukedom. He did not even call himself, as others called him, Count Othmar, and he put neither coronet or escutcheon on his carriages, his plate, or his writing-paper. He was far too proud to be proud in that way.

Illustrious alliances had been proposed to him, but he had rejected all; the world expected him to marry greatly, but he remained the hope and the despair of all the European nobilities, who would have willingly accorded him any one of their fair virgins. Their eagerness had early given him a cynical disdain for the aristocracies to which his tastes attracted him; he had no less a disdain for the financial order to which tradition allied him. On the whole, although he had never had any especial sorrow, he was scarcely a happy man, though the whole world was ready to gratify and amuse him.

He had been always able to indulge his fancies to the uttermost, but all the venal beauty which affected adoration for him left his heart cold.

Though gentle in manner and chary of speech, he could on provocation say caustic truths which cut like surgeons' knives. In general, however, he was indulgent to follies which he did not share. He lived always a little apart from the world in which he was so conspicuous a figure, and he judged it with good nature rather than with sympathy.

Occasionally, as Nadine Napraxine had said, *il voyait en jaune*; the bitterness of spirit which comes over all who see themselves sought for what they possess passed over him also, but its pessimism never lasted long. That human nature was trivial but not evil was, on the whole, the result of his experiences.

By one of the odd caprices in which destiny delights, a lettered ease would have been the utmost he would have cared to command. The incessant demands which a great fortune always brings upon its possessor were to him irksome; wherever he went mankind pursued him hat in hand and hand outstretched. He could arrive nowhere without petitions and invitations raining in on him; obscurity was not to be enjoyed even in Mongolia, where the Foreign Ministers at the Chinese Court and the Celestial Emperor himself sent mounted messengers after him to see that he came to no harm. The interest everywhere excited by his arrival or by his actions irritated him perpetually; the impossibility of securing privacy, to him formed the gravest of annoyances. His intolerance of publicity made him almost detest the whole human race which combined to refuse it to him. To be compelled to live in a glass-house appeared to him to destroy the very first requisite for life's enjoyment. He concealed this sensitiveness under a chilliness of manner which did injustice to the real warmth of his sympathies. There was much that was at once attractive and irritating to women in this young man whose fortunes were so immense and power so extended, who yet passed through the world with so unaffected an indifference to his own advantages in it, and who had the melancholy and romantic features of a Ruy Blas or of a Rolla. With men, his perfect simplicity of expression, his unpretentious courage, and his unfailing generosity, commanded respect, whilst his position excited their envy; but while he compelled their esteem, he did not, as a rule, possess their attachment. 'If we are in a position to serve men greatly, we shall never be greatly loved by them,' said Melville to him once; 'we shall make too many ingrates, even though we do our best not to make one. Men, as a rule, love most what they can afford a little to despise and have no cause whatever to envy. Do you remember when the anarchists of '48 came to old Rothschild at Ferrières and demanded his fortune for the people of France, and he very quietly took up his pen and made aloud his calculation that his fortune divided thus would give everyone just four francs and a half each? Well, the fault of the very rich man to the world is always Rothschild's to the anarchists; everyone expects he can bestow on each of them ten millions, whilst he can only really give four francs and a half. The calculation may be as clear as day, but the fact is one never forgiven.'

Othmar understood that very well with his reason, but he was not reconciled to it in his heart; he would have desired something different. The immense hotel which his father had built, with its ceilings painted by Ingres and Delaroche, its gardens sloping to the Seine, its genuine treasures of art, its double staircase, its *cour d'honneur*, its stables built on the model of Chantilly, was no better than a barn to him; he detested it with a sort of petulance; he never willingly resided in it. Its network of communication with the banks and the bureaux, laid with all the facilities which modern science could invent, had no interest for him. He did not feel the slightest emotion about any public event that could possibly happen, whether wars and rumours of wars, or the betting of a racecourse. He had none of those tastes which may make a rich man popular for a season and ruined in a twelvemonth. To his mistresses he was invariably generous, but these extravagances scarcely made more impression on his vast fortune than a few pailsfull taken from the sea make diminution in its volume. His greatest pleasure, on which he spent his money most largely, was music. Wherever he was he gathered great singers and musicians around him. She had likened him to Ludwig of Bavaria. His caprices were not quite so eccentric, but his preference was almost as ungrudgingly indulged. He had studied music theoretically and profoundly, though he had never touched any instrument and had never written a bar. It was one of those tastes which to his father had appeared an absolute insanity. He also spent much upon his libraries and his horses, as the Princess Napraxine had said to him. But since he was not a bibliophile, and did not care for rare editions, and never raced or made wagers, his expenditure even here was moderate as compared with his powers. From the time of his early and bitter passion for Sara Vernon he had avoided those famous sorceresses who can beggar Crœsus and discrown Cæsar; they recalled too vividly to him the intense suffering of his boyhood, when he had found himself betrayed by what he adored. To the few women whom he had ever noticed he had been invariably generous even to excess, with a generosity that strove to make amends for the scorn he had for them; but he had had none of those long-enduring *liaisons* which cling like the octopus and drain like the vampire. The knowledge that so many women would have drunk the dregs of infamy at his word for the sake of his gold, held him aloof from them; he was conscious that they pursued him as the sword-fish pursues the fish entangled in a seine. There was no Venusburg which would not have let him enter into its enchantment with his golden key; and this untempted

Tannhäuser turned away indifferent. All the rest which attracted other men—gambling, feasting, drinking, racing, living together in feverish crowds,—appeared to him ridiculous and tiresome. All the popular vices of men of his rank seemed to him dull and vulgar, trivial and stupid; the life of the *muscadin*, of the masher, seemed to him, on the whole, more stupid than the Tartar's. There was a certain similarity between him and Nadine Napraxine. The world appeared to them both very narrow and its resources few.

For her the result of this impression took the shape of disdain; in him of regret.

In her it was a thirst of the mind, in him it was a hunger of the heart, which led them to think that the land around them was barren.

His friends called him jestingly as Chateaubriand was called, '*le grand ennuyé*,' but it was precisely his vague discontent with the puerilities and the vulgarities of existence which made his affinity to Nadine Napraxine. She had much the same contempt for all those who surrounded her and who made so much of all their little ambitions, who crowned themselves with straw and thought they reigned, who set their souls on a winning horse, a political measure, a policy, a project, or a *coup d'état*, whilst the horse was to her taste as much worth wasting thought on as the statesmanship.

If he had heard of his own total ruin he would have put a Horace in his pocket and walked out of the great bronze Renaissance gates of his palace with a serenity which would have had in it nothing either strained or affected. He was no ascetic or philosopher, but his great fortunes bored him, and their origin annoyed him. His temperament would probably have led to higher ambitions if he had not been born to so much possession that ambition had no scope. He was wont to cite as the wisest man the world had known the gay physician of the Fronde epoch, Gui Patin, who sat throughout that troublous time, peaceful and amused, beneath his own cherry-trees. But fate had seated him, himself, beneath the gold pagoda-tree, and the tree seemed to him a sterile one; it had neither fragrance nor shade, yet a million eager hands were always trying to pluck from it, and for him who sat under it there was no quiet. Some one was always wanting him to shake down the fruit into their hands.

He had had one great misfortune; he had known satiety almost before he had known enjoyment; and men were so bent upon making use of him that they did not take time to attach him to them before they disgusted him. The world in general did not like him much; it followed him endlessly, but it thought his reserve arrogance, his simplicity of taste affectation, and his dislike to display avarice. It did not comprehend in the least the simple truth that Othmar would have shaken his gold off him if he could have done so like so much mud. In the Croat character there are both romance and religion; he had more of the Croat than the English temper in him; but, like most men of his time, he had no belief at all, though it was a sorrow to him, not a boast; and the romance of his impulses had been early chilled and silenced by the venal passions offered to his boyhood for sake of his wealth. He learned too early that there is scarcely anything which may not be bought. It is a knowledge which hardens the selfish, but saddens the generous, nature. The irresistible conviction that money is after all the one great power of the world is not an exhilarating or a consoling fact for thoughtful or visionary minds.

He knew very well that he might have been the most vicious brute, the most brutal tyrant, the most merciless of men, and mankind would have served, followed, and flattered him none the less; he could have purchased immunity for most crimes, condonation for most iniquities. So long as he had remained master of his fortune and of his possessions, he knew that men would have sought him none the less eagerly though he had had the vices of a Heliogabalus; and that women would have given themselves to him none the less willingly though he had been as hideous as the Veiled Prophet. It did not make him cynical; but it made him indifferent, and it moved him at times to a vague sadness. It seemed scarcely worth while for his forefathers to have raised that mountain of gold, only that from its summit he might see the nakedness of the world of men.

———————

# CHAPTER VII.

At eight o'clock on the following night Othmar walked across his gardens, under a starlit sky, towards the adjacent grounds of Millo. A few roods of plantation parted his from theirs; in the boundary fence there was a small gate, of which his major-domo had reminded him that a key existed. The night was young, but the stars already were many, and a slender moon had risen in the deep serene blue of the heavens. Though it was midwinter the air was sweet with the smell of orange orchards in flower and of the aromatic pine-woods of his own enclosures.

'Will she be there?' he thought a hundred times.

He had kept away from her all the day, had busied himself with his sailors, with his steward, with the condition of the place; but he longed to see that smile which even in its malice was sweeter to him than all the kindness of others, to hear again that voice which was music to his ear, even in its chill, indifferent mockeries.

He had an intuitive belief, which had been shaken but not destroyed by his own failure, that in her nature there were depths to be reached, passions to be awakened, though a bland and cruel indifference at present veiled them. He had been ruthlessly betrayed by her coquetry, profoundly wounded by her coldness, but he believed in her still—even still believed in himself as the man whom ultimately she would love. He had returned to Europe with the resolution never to be in her presence except when the hazards of society should bring them perforce in the same atmosphere, but at the first charm of her regard he had forgotten all his resolves, lost all his wisdom. Life only seemed worth living if he could hear that one voice, so sweet in its modulations, so chilly in its perfect harmony. It was, perhaps, because he was one of the few men who could gratify all wishes, caprices, and ambitions as fast as such arose, that this one thing wholly denied to him, wholly inaccessible, had such force of attraction for him. Yet he was bitterly angered against himself for his own submission. She was but a supreme coquette, a woman *pétrie du monde*, despite all her charm; but she could make her careless little nod, or a half-ironical smile, more prized from her than the utmost tenderness of other women ever was. There was about her that air as of one so wholly indifferent to all the vulgarities which others esteem triumphs that, when she ever deigned to notice that a man existed, he was more flattered than by the fondest concessions of his most ardent adorers. She had been assailed by all the powers and vanities of passion, but she had always given it at most that cool little smile—sometimes the smile had been compassionate, more often it had been cruel. Women had succumbed to him as full-blown roses fall before the touch of a careless hand; for this reason the chillness of Nadine Napraxine, which seemed chastity, had had so strong an attraction for him that for awhile it had seemed to him sweeter to wait upon its caprices than to obtain fuller response from them. But no man tarries long at this stage of his affections, and the time had come when he had grown impatient of a pursuit without end, of an allegiance without recompense. It was like an empty cup of exquisite form and transparent beauty, for ever without wine in it; to the connoisseur the gem is perfect thus, but to those athirst it brings little delight.

The unshuttered windows of Millo were glistening with light, which shone through the thickets of rose-laurel and bay as he approached the house, and a flood of light was poured out shining on the stone *perron*, carpeted and screened closely by rose-coloured awnings from the air of night. After a year and a half spent on tropic seas and in desert lands, the return to society has always a half-sweet, half-bitter, flavour. Was it worth while, he thought, to leave all the routine and tedium and emptiness of the world only to drift back again into its formalities and follies?

He had, however, no choice left in the matter, for the servants in the antechamber were bowing low to him and taking his furred coat from him, and in another moment the Duchesse de Vannes was welcoming him with all the genuine pleasure which a hostess feels in having the first visit from a person long absent, and high enough in the world's favour to make his return to the world an event of social interest and of public importance.

Aurore de Vannes, called Cri-Cri by her friends, was a very pretty woman, as much and as delicately painted as the fan she carried; she wore a marvellous costume of cream-coloured velvet blent with japonica-coloured satin, and had japonicas in her hair and at her bosom; she wore also some very fine rubies.

When he entered the drawing-rooms of Millo there were a dozen persons assembled there, most of whom he knew, but amongst them was not the Princess Napraxine. There was lamentation for her absence, but no surprise at it, because her caprices were so well known.

As he entered a little note had entered behind him; when Mme. de Vannes had said all her pretty greetings to him she glanced at it.

"'Désolée—migraine—temps détestable,'" she murmured, as she ran her eyes over it. 'Of course!' she said, aloud, 'that is always Nadine's way—she does it on purpose. She loves to disappoint people. She was out riding this afternoon; I saw her in the distance with Boris Seliedoff. She treated the Empress in that fashion last winter at Petersburg, and when the Dames du

Palais told her that the Tsarina was so displeased that she would exclude her from Court, Nadine said to them quite simply: "Trop de bonté! Je m'habitue si mal à ces corvées-là."'

'And has she been excluded?' asked one of the guests.

'Ouf!' cried the Duchesse de Vannes, 'I see you do not know her. No empress in the world would dare to exclude her. Imagine how she would avenge herself! Courts cannot afford to be brave nowadays.'

Othmar heard every syllable she said as he conversed with De Vannes, a tall man of some eight-and-thirty years old, with a look of extreme distinction and of as supreme fatigue. 'Who is Boris Seliedoff?' he thought, with the restless jealousy of an unsatisfied passion. He regretted his tent in Tartary: the elegant rooms, the perfumed air, the pretty women, the low buzz of conversation, the little breaks of laughter, the artificiality, the monotony of the whole thing, wearied him already.

The dinner was gay and even brilliant; to him alone it seemed tedious. Why had she not come? he thought, and that disappointment alone occupied him. He was angered that she should have so much power to make *la pluie et le beau temps* of his time and of his moods.

'Is Othmar cured by Central Asia?' said one of the guests to the Duchesse de Vannes who looked across the table at him, and answered, 'I should say not. He would hardly be within five leagues of La Jacquemerille if he were so. Besides, Nadine has a power of making herself remembered which I have seen in no one else. It is because she remembers nothing herself. The law of contrasts is the law of affinity.'

'Madame Napraxine is the only woman in whom virtue does not look ridiculous,' said an old gentleman to his neighbour, overhearing her name. 'But then, true, this is because it is not virtue at all, but something much more disdainful and unapproachable. Have you seen a peacock ravage a flower-garden? He does not care for any one of the flowers, but all the same the carnations and roses and geraniums fall in showers as he goes, strewing them right and left, and drawing his plumes carelessly over the waste he has made behind him. Her lovers are no more to Madame Napraxine than the flowers to the peacock; but the result is the same.'

'Is that a quality you would rank very highly?' asked the person next him.

'That depends on your standard,' he answered. 'It is a power which is to her just what plumage is to the peacock—something quite beyond imitation, and royal in its disdainful beauty. I did not think men were ever hopelessly in love in this century, but with her I perceive that they are so.'

'Othmar'—— began the other.

'Othmar?' repeated the old diplomat, 'Othmar reminds me of a man I once knew, who was a collector of miniatures; the collection has been dispersed now by unworthy heirs, but some twenty years ago it was a marvel of completeness. Every admirable miniaturist whom the world has possessed was represented in it by his finest examples. It had taken him thirty-five years and more millions to make it what it was. Any one else would have thought it perfect. He did not, because he had not an example amongst it of Karl Huth. You may never have heard of Karl Huth; I never had. He was a German miniaturist of the sixteenth century; he dwelt at Daunenberg, a small place on the Elbe. There is nothing of him in any museum, and there was supposed to be nothing of him anywhere but his tradition. For thirty-five years my friend hunted North and South Germany for a Karl Huth. At length, such was his perseverance that he did find an undeniable Karl Huth, in the family of a tradesman at Grieffenhagen, in a little portrait of a woman, on ivory, the size of a walnut, and signed and dated. His joy was immense; but, alas! it was of short duration. The burgomaster who owned it would not part with it. My friend offered sums untold for this three inches of ivory, would have sold his estates to purchase it, stopped at nothing in his frantic offers; but the burgomaster was rich, too, and inflexible; he would not sell the Karl Huth. There was some fable in his family about it. Two obstinacies met with a shock like the foreheads of two elephants in combat; of course the Teuton obstinacy beat the Gaul's. The Karl Huth remained in the burgomaster's possession, and my friend had such an excess of rage and despair that it brought on gout and killed him in an inn in that obscure Pomeranian town—all because with three thousand five hundred famous miniatures he failed to acquire one obscure example. Now Madame Napraxine is certainly not obscure, nevertheless she is the Karl Huth of Othmar. He is one of those men who can command and enjoy everything; therefore, of course, he has set his heart on the only woman, probably, in Europe who will not smile on him. All his grand collection became worthless to my poor friend when once he failed to include in it that single Karl Huth.'

Othmar, meanwhile, unconscious that they talked of him, even unconscious that his passion for his friend's wife had been ever suspected by his world, found the dinner tedious, and was not distracted by his neighbours, both of whom were lovely women.

When they returned to the salons at the further end of the great central drawing-room, which was all white and silver, with satin panels embroidered with silver thread, and doors made of mirrors painted with groups of flowers, there was seated all alone at one of the little tables a very young girl, who wore a plain white gown, with a plain black sash tied around her waist, *à l'enfant*, and a black ribbon holding up the thick masses of her fair hair.

'That is Cendrillon,' thought Othmar, moved to a vague interest as he recalled the story which Melville had told; and he looked on her more attentively.

As she rose at the entrance of the Duchess he saw that she was very tall for her age; the slim, straight, unornamented frock became her: she had neither awkwardness nor self-consciousness, neither much timidity nor any self-assertion. There was a look about her of spirited but restrained life which was pathetic, the look of any high-couraged young animal which is too early and too rudely tamed.

'Poor child!' thought Othmar in an involuntary pity, as he saw the Duchess go up to her, tap her carelessly on the shoulder with a fan, present her to another lady and with that other lady turn away indifferently after a few words. The girl curtsied low with perfect grace, and resumed her seat; she appeared used to be forgotten. She sat quite still, neither embarrassed by neglect or solicitous of attention. She might have been a statue but for her half-veiled eyes, of a luminous golden brown shaded by long black lashes, and her mouth like a rose, which had made him call her a Greuze picture as she had passed him in the boat. She had looked much happier in the boat than she looked now in the drawing-room.

Othmar watched her a little while. No one approached her: the men present did not care for *ingénues*; the women, it is needless to say, cared still less. The Duchesse did not think it necessary to trouble herself about a child who was still in a convent and would soon be in one for the rest of her days. She was not averse to such an evidence of her own charity as her young cousin presented sitting there, carefully dressed, admirably educated, in living testimony of the benevolence of Aurore de Vannes; but there was no need for more than the tap with the fan and the good-natured indifferent *Comment va-t-on ce soir, petite?*

Othmar waited some ten or twelve minutes, then approached his hostess.

'Duchesse, will you do me the honour to present me to Mdlle. de Valogne?'

She stared at him in astonishment.

'Certainly—yes; why not?—But how did you know her name? And she is only a child at Sacré Cœur.'

'Melville told me her sad little story and of all your amiability towards her. Surely she will soon be a very beautiful woman?'

'*Elle n'est pas mal*,' said the Duchess, somewhat irritably. 'Melville is always romancing, you know; there is nothing to be romantic about; she is destined to the religious life; it was her grandmother's wish, and is her own. As for presenting you to her, she is only a child; it would not be well to make her think herself in the world. If you would excuse me———'

'Pray present me, Duchesse,' he persisted. 'I assure you I do not eat children; and if she be doomed to take the veil so soon, the world will lose her anyhow. But will you have the heart to cut off all that hair?'

'You will always have your own way,' said Madame de Vannes, who knew very well that he did not have it where most he cared; then she took him across to where her young cousin sat, and said, 'Yseulte, Count Othmar wishes to know you; he is a friend of Monsignor Melville's.'

The girl made him the same grand curtsy, which she had made before, only a little less low than she had given to the lady. Then she seated herself once more, and waited for him to speak first, as we wait for a royal person to do so.

He spoke to her of Melville, divining that the way to her confidence would be through his regard for the early period of her childhood. She listened with pleasure to his praises of her grandmother's friend, and answered him in few syllables; but the restraint seemed to him the result neither of timidity nor of want of intelligence, but of the reserve which had been imposed upon her alike at her convent and here at Millo, where no one heeded her unless the Duc threw her a good-natured glance, or the Duchesse a petulant word of censure. It was easy to see that on a nature formed for light and laughter, the sense of being unneeded and undesired in the home of others had early cast shadows too deep for childhood.

'How very handsome she is!' he thought, as he spoke of Melville and his many noble works. Close to her he could see the exceeding regularity of her features, the splendour of her eyes, the purity of her complexion, which was not the narcissus whiteness of Nadine Napraxine, but that childlike fairness under which the colour mantles at any passing thought, or any effort or exercise. Her form, too, had all the slenderness and indecision of youth, but it had also the certainty of a magnificent womanhood. Her low dress showed her white shoulders, her quickly-breathing childlike breast, her beautiful throat.

'All that to be wasted in a cloister!' he thought, with repugnance. It seemed a sin against nature's finest work, youth's most gracious grace. To be sixteen years old, and to have a face as fair as a flower, and to be the last of a great race, and yet to be doomed to be joyless, loverless, childless, from birth unto death, because a little gold and silver were lacking to her! To the master of millions it seemed the cruelest irony of fate that he had ever encountered. Why should the absurd codes and prejudices of the world make him powerless to give this unhappy child out of his abundance the little which she would need to take her place amidst those common human joys which the poorest can attain, but which the selfishness of man and the customs of society forbade to her, merely because she had been nobly born? He was thinking of her fate all the while that he talked to her of Melville; he was thinking of that supple slender form disguised under the nun's heavy garb, of that abundant hair shorn and falling to the stone floor. Could those gay, good-natured, idle, spendthrift people who condemned her so lightly to such a sacrifice, not surrender one of their luxuries, one of their follies, to save her?

Then he pictured to himself, with a smile at his own whimsical conceit, the tailors' bills of Madame de Vannes curtailed, her caprices sacrificed, her equipages diminished, her *parties de chasse* discontinued, her superfluous jewels sold, to furnish with the result attained a dower to her portionless cousin! These good people called themselves Christians; nevertheless, such generosity would have seemed to them as impossible as to go out on to the boulevards in the goatskin of John the Baptist. Would there ever be a religion that should influence the lives of its professors? Christianity had had its own way for nigh two thousand years, and had scarcely left a mark on the world so far as practical renunciation went.

While he mused thus, he talked lightly and kindly to the girl, but he met with little response. The convent education had taught her silence, and she thought that he had only come to her side because he had pitied her solitude; that thought made her shy and proud. With all his good will, he failed to make much way into her friendship, or to elicit much more than monosyllabic replies, and he would have felt his benevolence wearisome had it not been that there was so much true loveliness in her features and in her form that he was not glad of his release when she was called by the Duchesse to the piano.

'Could you make anything of Yseulte?' said the Duc de Vannes to him. 'She is the true *ingénue* of the novelist and dramatist; she knows nothing beyond the four walls of the convent. It is a type fast disappearing, even with us, under the influence of American women and English romances. I am not sure that it is not to be regretted; it is something, at least, to have a girlhood like a white rose.'

'But you are going to set the rose to wither before the sanctuary of Marie?' said Othmar, still moved by his one idea.

The Duc shrugged his shoulders.

'Oh, that is my wife's affair. Myself, I think it is a pity. The child will be a magnificent woman; but then, you see, she has no dower. Where can she go except to the cloisters? Listen! she sings well.'

She was singing then, and her voice rose with singular richness, like the notes of a nightingale smiting the silence of a golden southern noon. The quality of her voice was pure and strong, with a sound in it as of unshed tears, of restrained, and perhaps unconscious, emotion.

'And she will only sing the *Laus Deo* and the *Kyrie Eleison*,' thought Othmar, 'and no one will hear her except a few scores of sad-hearted, stupid women, who will succeed in making her as sad-hearted and as stupid as themselves!'

What she rendered was the sweetest of all the simple Noëls written by Roumanille, the song of the blind child who begs her mother to take her to see the Enfant Jésus in the church, and to whom the mother long replies, in chiding and hardness of heart: 'What use, since thou canst not see?' Saint-Saëns had set the naive and pathetic words to music which was penetrated with that *esprit provençal* which has in it 'les pleurs du peuple et les fleurs du printemps;' and the voice of the girl was pure, tender, and solemn, in unison with what she treated.

'Je sais qu'au tombeau seul finit ma voie obscure;

Je sais encor

Que je ne verrai pas, divine créature,

Ta face d'or.

'Mais qu'est-il besoin d'yeux pour adorer et croire?

Si mes yeux sont

A te voir impuissants, mes mains, ô Dieu de gloire,

Te toucheront!'

L'aveugle à ses genoux pleure si fort, et prie

Sur un tel ton,

D'un air si déchirant, que la mère attendrie

N'a plus dit non.

Oh! comme la pauvrette, en entrant dans la grotte,

En tressaillait!

De Jésus sur son cœur elle mit la menotte:

Elle voyait!

Of all those who listened to her, the old minister, who had spoken of Karl Huth, and Othmar himself, were the only persons touched by the likeness of the words of the Noël to the destiny which awaited the singer of it.

'Je sais qu'au tombeau seul finit ma voie obscure,'

Othmar repeated to himself. 'Poor child! there will be no miracle wrought for her.'

It seemed to him pathetic, and even cruel.

She had sung with science and accuracy which were in contrast with the very youthful cadence of her voice, and when she ceased there was a murmur of applause. She blushed a little, and with a composure that was almost dignity accepted the compliments paid her, and went back, without a word, to her seat.

'She would make a name for herself as an artist if she were not the last Comtesse de Valogne,' thought Othmar. 'Poor child! it is hard to bear all the harness and curb of rank and have none of its gilded oats to eat.'

A pretty *élégante* was now singing a song of Judic's with even more suggestion by gesture and of glance than the original version of it gave; the air of the drawing-room rippled with her silvery notes and their response of subdued laughter; everyone forgot Mdlle. de Valogne and the Provençal Noël. When Othmar looked again for her, she was gone: the salon saw her no more that night.

'You were soon tired, Othmar,' said the Duchesse. 'Naturally: what should you find to say to a child from a convent? She has not two ideas.'

'She speaks little, certainly,' he answered; 'but I am not sure that it is from want of ideas; and even if she have no ideas, what does a beautiful woman want with them?—and she is beautiful.'

'I thought you liked clever women.'

'Clever! Oh, what a comprehensive word. It is like that balloon they advertise, which you can either fold up in your pocket or float as high as the moon. As for Mdlle. de Valogne, I should think she was very intelligent, to judge by her brow and her eyes. But convents do not nourish their pupils on Rénan and Huxley.'

'Rénan?' said the Duchess, with a charming affectation of ignorance. 'Oh, that is the man who writes so many volumes about himself to explain why he cannot bring himself to believe some story about an almond bough that swallowed snakes! When Voltaire began that sort of thing, it seemed shocking, but it was new; nowadays it is not new and nobody is shocked; it is only tiresome.'

'But you, Madame, who laugh, yet respect the Church enough to sacrifice a virgin to it as the Greek to the Minotaur?'

'There is no other retreat possible for girls of good family who are portionless,' said the Duchess very positively.

'But there are many men who do not marry for a dower.'

'Perhaps, but not with us; it would be quite impossible, an unheard of thing,' said the Duchesse, scandalised at such a suggestive violation of all etiquette and family dignity.

From time immemorial the younger sons or the unmarriageable daughters of the Valogne, of the Creusac, of the d'Authemont, of all the great races whose blood met in this child, had hidden their narrowed fates with decorum and stateliness in the refuge of the cloisters; why should she, because she had been born in the latter half of the nineteenth century, rebel against so just a disposal? And she did not rebel at all, would not, unless some man made love to her and put rebellion in her head. That man would not be Othmar; he had only one thought—Nadine Napraxine. If she had not been sure of that, she would not even have presented him to her young cousin, for she was a very proud woman despite her frivolity, and to seek a rich alliance for a poor relative would have seemed to her the last of degradations. Her own people, and her husband's, had always married as sovereigns do, accepting and conferring equal advantages.

'Poverty has the right to be as proud as it chooses so long as it accepts nothing; when once it has accepted anything, it has become mendicity,' had said often the old Marquise de Creusac to her granddaughter, and Yseulte would not do dishonour to that lesson.

'One can trust her implicitly,' said Madame de Vannes once to her husband, who had answered:

'Oh, yes, my dear; that is the result of an old-fashioned education. When your Blanchette and Toinon are at her age, they will know everything objectionable under the sun, but they will not let you know that they know it. You are bringing them up *more britannico!*'

# CHAPTER VIII.

Yseulte de Valogne, waking the next morning and looking through the little panes of her high window in the roof at the landscape which the red leaves of the Canadian vine framed in crimson, was conscious of a new interest in her life. Some one, she did not know whom, for in her confusion she had not heard his name, had spoken to her with kindness, and that deference to her incipient womanhood which is the sweetest flattery to a very young girl. Othmar, with the grace of his manner, the seriousness and coldness which made him different to the men of his time, and his handsome features, to which an habitual reserve had given that expression of self-control and of melancholy which most attracts her sex, had seemed to her imagination like some gracious knight of old bending to pity her loneliness, and to succour that timidity which was in so much due to her pride and her unwillingness to be regarded with compassion and to her dread lest she should seem to seek attention.

She thought of him with a vague personal interest stronger than any she had felt in her simple and monotonous life, since her childhood on the Ile St. Louis had become to her like an old book of prayer, shut up unused, with the lavender and southern-wood of long dead summers faded and dried inside it. Though she was only sixteen, that childhood seemed so far, so very far, away. It would have appeared to Blanchette and Toinon, with their artificial, excited, *blasé* little lives, a dull and austere childhood enough, passed beside the infirmities and incapacities of age, and with no other active pleasure than to gather marguerites on the grass islands of the Seine or to hear a Magnificat sung at Notre Dame.

The rooms they lived in had been narrow and dark, their food had been of the simplest, their days regulated with exact and severe precision. But she had been so happy! When her grandmother, with the white hair like spun silk and the thin small hands, on which one great diamond sparkled—sole relic of a splendid past—said, with a smile, 'C'est bien fait, mon enfant,' all the universe could have added nothing to her content.

When the old man servant Bénoît had taken her out to the Sainte Chapelle, or the graves at the Abbaye, and had told her tales of how her forefathers had died on the scaffold, in the *noyades*, on the battle-fields of Jemappes, or in the slaughter of Quiberon, she had known that purest of all pride, which rejoices in the honour and loyalty of the dead who have begotten us. All the air about her had been redolent of fidelity, of courage, of dignity. She had breathed in that fine clear atmosphere of integrity as the transparent dianthus drinks in the sea-water which the sunbeams pierce with vivifying gold. When the Marquise had sometimes taken, out of old sandal-wood coffers, antique brocades, dusky old jewels, faded yellow letters, perhaps a ribbon and a star of some extinct order once worn at Marly or at Amboise, the child had listened with reverent ear and beating heart to the stories which went with the relics and keepsakes, and it had always seemed to her as if some perfume of the past entered her very veins, as its fragrance is poured upwards from the root into the flower. Nor had it been always melancholy, that innocent, tranquil life; gentlemen of the old courtly habits had made their bow humbly in those narrow rooms, and the old *gaieté gauloise* had laughed sometimes beneath the sad serenity of losses nobly borne. There had been merry days when Bénoît had taken her in one of the boats which crossed the Seine in summer, and had rowed to one of those quiet nooks of which he had the secret, and had landed with her amidst the tall hay grasses, and had set her noonday meal there—a little fruit and roll of bread—watching the poplars quiver in the light, and the women work upon the shore, and the clumsy brown brigs come and go on the broad breast of the river; and she had clasped a great sheaf of may and daisies and kingcups in her arms, and had run hither and thither in a very ecstasy of limbs set free and eyes delighted, and had cried her delight aloud to the old man, who had nodded and smiled and said, 'Oui, oui, c'est beau,' but had thought, with a pang at his faithful heart, 'Si jeunesse savait——.'

Then, whilst she was still a young child, there had fallen across her life the darkness of the 'année terrible.' The Marquise de Creusac had been at once too brave and too poor to quit Paris when the wall of iron and of fire had closed in around it. Her sons had died, one at the cavalry charge of Fræschweiler, the other during the siege of Strasburg; she herself never rose from her bed during that ghastly winter, and her last breath left her lips as the Prussians entered Paris. The horror of that time could never wholly pass from the mind of Yseulte. Bénoît had travelled with her to the château of Bois les Rois, and placed her under the roof of her only living relative, Aurore de Vannes, who herself was momentarily saddened and touched by the misfortunes of the country and the loss of many of her kinsmen, and in that chastened mood was kinder to the little friendless fugitive than she might have been at another and less desperate time.

All that time seemed very far away to Yseulte now; to earliest youth, a few years seems like the gap of a century.

Bénoît was dead now, like the mistress he had adored and served, with that loyal service which, in this later time, one class has lost the power to inspire and the other class has lost the capacity to render; but those happy midsummer holidays on the islets of the Seine were always in her mind whenever she felt the touch of the fresh air or smelt the scent of growing leaves. They had spread a fragrance like that of summer all over her memories of childhood. She pitied Blanchette and Toinon, who cared nothing for daisies and kingcups; who tired so soon of their costly playthings; who knew their Trouville and Biarritz by heart, who, when they played at their games, were either peevish or bored, and who looked with all the scorn of fashionable eight-year-olders on a toilette which was a season out of date. Blanchette and Toinon would die without ever having been young; their cousin, who at sixteen was still entirely a child, had to die to the world before she had begun to live.

She leaned out of her window in the chill of the early morning, and she watched the sea mists curl up and drift away before the sun, the mountains come forth slowly from the clouds obscuring them, the light touch and reveal one by one the low white bastides, the grey olive yards, the bosquets of orange and lemon, the fields where the young corn already was spreading, the fantastic buildings which diversified and vulgarised the beauty of the scene, and the grey towers of S. Pharamond sober and severe amidst its ilex woods by contrast with the coquetteries and motley phantasies of its neighbours.

'I wonder,' she thought for the hundredth time, 'if it were only because he pitied me that he talked to me?'

She went on wondering who he was, what he was; she did not even know that he owned S. Pharamond, and dared ask no one about him; all the gay, thoughtless, inquisitive questions which youth loves to put, whilst often too impatient to wait for an answer to them, had been too perpetually frozen on her lips for silence not to have become a second nature to her.

'What you can observe is well,' her grandmother had often said to her; 'it is the wheat you have gleaned, and you have a right to it. But never gain knowledge by asking questions; it is the short cut across the fields which only trespassers take.'

At the convent any interrogations which she had been tempted to make had been repressed as too apposite to be convenient, and of the Duchesse de Vannes she would have no more have asked a question or a favour than she would have asked one of the lay figures on which the Duchesse's marvellous costumes were built up, bit by bit, as idea succeeded to idea in the brains of great artists of the toilette.

She had scarcely heard a dozen sentences from Madame Aurore in the half-dozen years through which she had spent her summer vacations at their great castle in the Vosges, a lonely place where she had usually only the house-servants as companions; but in winter at Millo she had been always happy, for near Millo dwelt her foster-mother, a Savoyarde, who had become well-to-do since the time when, a poor young unwedded mother astray on the mercy of Paris, she had been glad to give her breast to the motherless child of the Comtesse de Valogne. Through the influence and aid of the Marquise de Creusac the woman Nicole had ultimately married her lover, a sturdy peasant of the environs of Nice, and by thrift and hard work and good luck and good husbandry combined, they now owned a bastide and an orange-orchard, and could receive 'la petite Comtesse' with honey and cream and conserves of their own manufactures. They had no children, and Mlle. de Valogne still filled in the heart of her foster-mother the place which had been empty and cold when a month-old baby had gasped out its last breath of feeble life in a Paris hospital sixteen years before.

'What is the good of it all, the *pétiot* is dead and gone?' said Nicole Sandroz many a time, looking over her hives and hen-houses, her rose-beds and her green peas, all blooming for the Paris market. But this mood was transient; the *pétiot* was not to be recalled by regret, and the solid delight of early vegetables and their value remained to her. She was a good woman, though hard in some ways and greedy; but she was the only creature who gave Yseulte de Valogne anything of the comfort of human affection and tender, blind, unreasoning admiration. To Nicole 'mon enfant la Comtesse' was an object of honest adoration, to be waited on, worshipped, petted, slaved for if need be; and this wholly sincere, if clumsy, devotion had always been to the starved heart of the girl as the one scrap of moss on the frozen sea and shore is to the lonely and lost voyager.

When the dark, hard-featured face of the Niçoise presented itself at the convent gates of Faïel, and with her load of oranges or strawberries, of camellias or roses, she came out of the hot sun into the quietness and dusk of the *parloir* and stretched out her big sturdy arms to her nursling, the proud eyes of Yseulte filled with tears as no one else ever saw them do. She was a little child once more clinging to her nurse's skirts in the old panelled rooms in the Ile St. Louis.

The low white walls of the bastide were set upon a hill-side not half-an-hour's walk from Millo, a fragrant, pleasant, homely place, with violets cultured like corn, and roses grown like currant-bushes, for the flower-shops of Paris and the purchase of the foreigners in Nice. The mere presence of Nicole made her visits to the southern shore longed for and enjoyed, and compensated to her for the fretful teazing of her little cousins, the ill-concealed enmity of their governesses, the perpetual sense of being undesired by any one there, and the many slights which the indifference of her hosts made them careless of inflicting. Aurore de Vannes would have said, if remonstrated with, that the girl could want for nothing. She had two pretty rooms all to herself, and a piano in one of them; had as many gowns as she could wear, though, of course, at her age they were the frocks of a *pensionnaire*; and could pass her time in the schoolroom or in the gardens very much at her pleasure; she could even drive out in the basket-carriage if Blanchette and Toinon did not want it. The existence must, she would have argued, at any rate be very much livelier than the convent.

In the first winter she had passed at Millo no one had come there but herself, and she had spent her time almost wholly with her foster-mother; later on, when the house was full—as it was now—she obtained in her holidays a large amount of liberty, from the fact that it was no one's especial duty to look after her. She used her freedom innocently enough, and always took the path under the olives which led to the flower-farm of the Sandroz.

Once the Duchesse had said to her irritably, 'What charm do you find in peasants grubbing among peastalks and growing salad?' But she had not waited for an answer, which was fortunate, as Yseulte would have been too shy to give the true one,—that they loved her a little.

The Duchesse concluded that the governesses of her children did their duty in attending on her young cousin. The governesses, however, were willing that one who was only an extra charge to them should do as she chose so long as she brought no trouble on themselves; few mornings passed without her finding her way to the welcome of her old nurse, to sit at pleasure under the shadow of the orange leaves, or drift through clear water in the big market boat.

Madame de Vannes was, as the world in general would have said, very generous to her; her education was of the best, the clothes provided for her were elegant and suitable, her linen was of the finest, her boots and shoes were the prettiest possible; the Duchesse did everything well that she did at all; but beyond a remark that her hair was too low or too high on her forehead, or that she did not wear the right gloves with the right frock, Yseulte could scarcely recall twenty phrases that she had heard from her august cousin. Now and then the heart of the girl had risen in an impulse of ardour towards liberty, towards independence. She was conscious of more talent than the manner of her education had developed; in a vague way she sometimes fancied the world might hold some place for her, some freedom of effort or attainment; but all the habits of obedience made a cage for her as surely as the laws made one. Her grandmother had written with a hand half paralysed by death to commend her to the care of her relative, and amongst her dying words the command: 'Obey Aurore as you have obeyed me,' had been often repeated. Any thought of rebellion was stifled by her sense of duty as soon as it arose.

This morning, as she leaned out of her window she could see the white house of the Sandroz, half a league away, amongst the olive foliage, and what was still more to her, the tiny bell tower of a little whitewashed church, the parish church of S. Pharamond, in whose parish Millo also lay. The one cracked bell sounding feebly for matins recalled her to the present hour, and reminded her that the morrow was the feast day of S. Cecilia to whom the building was dedicated.

'He will be so vexed if the altar be not dressed,' she thought. The old priest of Millo was accustomed to look to her for that service. The Duchesse always gave him two thousand francs in gold for his poor at New Year, but there her heed of her vicar ended. Yseulte, who had no gold to give, brought him flowers and boughs for his little, dusky, lonely place, where only a few fishermen and peasants ever knelt, and she sometimes sang at his Offices.

When she remembered the day, she wasted no more time at the window; she drank the cup of milk and ate the roll which the maid appointed to her service brought, and putting on a little hat of fur, went out through the house where even Blanchette and Toinon were still asleep, and only a few of the under servants were stirring.

It was cold, but already grown bright, with sunshine, and the promise of a warm noonday.

The gardens of Millo, with their autumn luxuriance still prolonged, were sparkling with sunbeams and dew-drops; their aloes and cacti pierced with broad sword-blades the blue clear air; the latest roses kissed the earliest camellias; the pink, the amber, the white, the purple, of groves of chrysanthemums, glowed in the parterres; but she did not dare to give them even a glance. No one ever plucked a flower there.

She went quickly through the alleys, and avenues, over the lawns, and under the *berceaux*, and after walking about a mile came to where the boundary of Millo was fixed by a high wall of closely-clipped arbutus, and only the small iron gate which Othmar had unlocked the previous night gave access to the lands of S. Pharamond, which lay beyond.

'There will be sure to be something here,' she thought, as she turned the latch of the gate which he had unthinkingly left open, and passed through the aperture into the thick ilex wood on the other side of the bearberry wall. She was not surprised to find it open, for the gardeners of the two houses often held communication; and she had been constantly permitted by those of S. Pharamond to wander about its grounds and pluck its commoner plants. It was a thing she had done a hundred times in the winters she had passed at Millo.

There were all kinds of plants growing up at Nicole's bastide; but as she had no money to pay, the child had always felt a delicacy in asking, for them. Her foster-mother would indeed have refused her nothing; but to take as a gift the late-come *quatre-saisons* rose, or the early-blooming *clochettes*, which the Sandroz could sell so highly by sending them away in little air-tight tin boxes to Paris, would have appeared to the generous temper of the last of the Valognes a very ungenerous act.

Othmar, who had slept ill, rose early that day. When he had bathed and dressed, he strolled out on to his terrace, where Nadine Napraxine had eaten her strawberries. Though winter, the morning was mild, the sunrise glorious. Through the great gloom of his ilex groves he could see the sparkle of blue waves. It was not the scenery he cared most for; he liked the great windy shadowy plains of eastern Europe, the snow of mountains more sombre and severe than these hyacinth-hued maritime Alps, the gigantic grey walls of Atlantic rollers breaking on rugged rocks of Spain, or Britanny, or Scotland; but he was not insensible to the present beauty which surrounded him, if it were brighter and paler of hue, gayer of tone, softer in character, than the scenes he preferred.

He stood and looked idly, and thinking, 'If I were wise I should go to Paris this morning.'

What was the use of letting all his years languish and drift aimlessly away for sake of a woman who made sport of his pain? Yonder, hidden by the curve of a distant cliff, was La Jacquemerille, and its mistress of the moment was, no doubt, sleeping soundly enough amongst the lace and cambric and satin of her bed, and would not have lain awake one moment thinking of him, though he had thought of her all night.

'Were people ever sleepless for love?' she had said once, with her pretty cynical smile. 'That must have been very long ago, before the chemists had given us chloral!'

As he stood and thus made his picture of her in his mind sleeping, as the narcissus which she resembled sleeps in the moonlight, he saw a figure underneath the ilex boughs which was not hers, but had a grace of its own, though wholly unlike her.

It was the figure of a girl in a grey close dress which defined the outline of her tall slim limbs. She wore a fur hat, and had some fur about her shoulders; the sunbeams of the early day touched the gold in her hair and shone in her hazel eyes. She was gathering now one datura, now another, of those spared by the December mistral, and coming up to a bed of camellias, paused doubtfully before their blossoms; she came there like one accustomed to the place, and who merely did what she had often done before. Her grey gown, her sunny hair under its crown of sable, her hands filled with flowers, made a picture underneath the palms, amidst the statues, against the ilex darkness.

He recognised the child whom he had last seen in her white gown with the black sash a few hours before in the Duchesse's drawing-rooms.

For the moment, he put on her appearance there that construction which a man, subject from his boyhood to the advances and solicitations of the other sex, was most apt to conceive of such an unsought visit. But as he saw how unconcerned, natural, and childlike her movements were as she paused, now by this shrub and now by that, or sat down on a bench to arrange some asters in her basket, he as rapidly discarded his suspicions and guessed the truth, that she had been ignorant of who he was the previous evening, and had come to his gardens by chance or by custom.

As he hesitated whether to descend and make her welcome, or to retreat unseen into the house and tell his servants to say nothing, she looked up and saw him. She dropped her flowers on the grass, and turned to run away like any startled nymph in classic verse, but he was too quick for her; he had descended the few steps from his terrace and had approached her before she could fly from him.

'Do not be so unkind to me,' he said, with deference and courtesy, for he divined how ashamed she was to have been found there. 'There is little in these gardens after being swept by the mistral, which is a cruel horticulturist, but the hothouses, I hope, may give you something worthier your acceptance.'

'I beg your pardon,' she murmured, 'there has been no one here so long——'

He had spoken as though her presence was the most natural thing in the world, but neither his composed acceptance of it or his courteous welcome could reconcile her to the position she occupied. She coloured painfully, and her breath came and went in an agitation she could not subdue.

'I beg your pardon,' she stammered again; 'I did not know—last night I did not hear your name—there has been no one here so long. Oh, what can you think of me!'

Her eyes were filled with sudden tears; her colour faded as suddenly as it had come. She was only a child, and had been reared by stern formalities and by chill precepts.

'Think?' echoed Othmar; 'that you are kind enough to treat me as a neighbour. Neighbours are not always friends, but I hope we shall be so.

That little gate has no use in it unless it be an open portal for friendship to pass to and fro; I walked through it to Millo last night.'

But his good nature and gentleness could not avail to console her for what was in her own eyes, as it would have been in that of her relatives, an unpardonable and infamous misdemeanour. Now that she recognised in the speaker the same person whom her cousin had presented to her the previous evening, she longed for the lawn she stood on to open and cover her. A piteous dismay took possession of her; would he ever believe that she had not known him as the owner of S. Pharamond? Would he ever believe that S. Pharamond had been that morning, as far as her knowledge had gone, still unoccupied as it had been for ten mortal years?

All the lessons of her convent life made her act appear in her own eyes one of inexcusable audacity, unspeakable horror,—to have come into the gardens of a stranger when he was himself there to take his flowers!

The kindness of his gaze and the cordiality of his welcome could do nothing to console her; she was barely conscious of them; the colour in her face mounted to the loose curls escaping from her little fur cap; she laid her basket down and joined her hands in an unconscious supplication.

'There has been no one here so long,' she said yet again with pathetic appeal in her voice. 'I thought I did no harm; M. Duvelleroy, the head gardener, has always let me come when there is a feast day. Indeed, I have never taken the rare flowers, only those which he did not want. It is the parish church of S. Pharamond, too; I did not know I did wrong—pray do not blame the gardeners.'

'Blame them, when I am so much their debtor! I wish you would believe that you are the queen of all the gardens here. Why, even still you are hesitating to pluck the camellias!'

'Because they told me never to touch them; I only looked at them; I think M. Duvelleroy sends them to Nice to sell. Indeed—indeed—I have never taken but what he told me I might have.'

What seemed so very terrible to her was that she must appear to the owner of S. Pharamond as a thief of his flowers! A vague idea flashed across her mind, that perhaps she might pay for the value of them—but then she had no money! The old jewels of her mother were to be hers, indeed; but when? She had not even seen them since her grandmother had died; perhaps they were to be sold to defray the cost of her entrance into convent life; she did not know. The great trouble of her spirit was reflected in her face, which was full of conflicting emotions; her mouth, which had been too silent the night before, trembled a little; the tears gleamed under her long lashes. Othmar thought her much more interesting with all this expression breaking up from under the mask of white marble which the convent had made her wear. In her bewilderment she became altogether a child; and the stately quiet of her manner fell away from her like an embroidered ermine-lined robe too heavy for her years.

'Do they sell my camellias—the rogues?' he said with a smile. 'Of course you shall go away if you will, but not empty-handed. There must be something better worth having than those frost-bitten roses.'

He called a man who was sweeping up leaves on a lawn here.

'Go and tell your chief to cut his finest orchids and bring them in a basket to me himself: any other rare thing he may have in the houses he can cut also. Mademoiselle,' he said, turning to the girl, 'you must not go back to Millo with such a poor opinion of my gardens. Is the Duchesse well? You remember that I had the honour to be presented to you by her last evening?'

'You are Count Othmar?'

'Men call me so,' he replied, for he never loved that title which seemed to him so contemptible a thing, given, as it had been, in the beginning of the century by the first Emperor. 'I am happy to be the owner of S. Pharamond, since you deign to visit it. You are at Millo every winter, I think?'

'I am; they are not,' she said, regaining her composure a little. 'I did not hear your name last night. I thought you were some gentleman from Paris.'

'I live oftenest in Paris,' he replied, 'but at the present moment I come from Central Asia. I am a friend of Monsignore Melville, as I told you; and I hope you will believe me when I say that, if only for his regard for you, you would be welcome at S. Pharamond.'

He spoke without compliment, seeing that any compliment would only scare her more.

'You help my parish church, did you say?' he continued. 'It is very disgraceful of me never to have known it; we will get Melville to come and preach there. Does the curé want for anything?—is there nothing I could do?'

'He wants a new *soutane* very much,' she said with hesitation.

'Then a new *soutane* he shall have before the world is a week older,' said Othmar. 'Why will you go away? Are you too afraid of me to venture into the house? Would you not have some cream, some cakes, some strawberries? What do young Graces like you live upon? Command anything you will.'

'I have had some bread and milk; I want nothing; you are very kind.'

'If you think me so, you must not treat me so distantly. You must make me a friend of yours. The Duchesse herself presented me last night. You seem determined to forget that.'

She stood inclined to go away, unwilling to seem ungrateful, yet afraid to remain; a charming picture of confusion and indecision, mingled with a gravity and a grace beyond her years. The Greuze face which he had seen in the boat bore the full force of the morning light as a rose bears it, the pure tints only deepened and illumined by it. Under the straight simple lines of the grey stuff gown the budding beauties of a still childish form could be divined; in her embarrassment her colour still came and went; her large eyes, of a golden hazel, were almost black from the shadow of their lashes. So far as a man whose heart and senses are engrossed by one woman can be alive to the loveliness of another, Othmar was sensible of this youthful and poetic beauty, which seemed to belong to the first fresh hours of the morning, and to be born of it as the rosebuds were.

'I hope you will not be angry,' she said anxiously. 'It was my fault. At Millo no one must touch a single flower, and the curé likes to see the altar pretty, and so one day—oh, that is quite a long time ago, three winters ago—I happened to see the gate open into these grounds, and I asked M. Henri if I might gather what he did not care to sell, and he said that I was welcome always to the common flowers. You will not blame him, if you please, for it was altogether my fault.'

She had seldom made a speech so long in her life, and she paused, ashamed of the sound of her voice in the quiet of the morning air. She feared also that she was doing wrong to speak at all to this stranger, all owner of S. Pharamond though he might be.

'All that I am inclined to blame him for,' answered Othmar, 'is for having laid any restrictions upon you; he has no right to sell even a sprig of mignonette. These gardens are not kept for profit; they can have no happier use than to contribute to your pleasure and to the altars of the church. Pray, do not go; wait a moment for this criminal to bring us the orchids.'

But she only grew more alarmed at her own intrusion there. The easy, kindly gallantry of his manner scarcely reassured her; she was but a child, and a child reared in formal and severe codes. She doubted that she was guilty of some grave offence in standing under a palm-tree beside a group of camellias with a person whom she had scarcely seen before. She had neither the habits of the world nor the conventional badinage which could have met his courtesy on its own ground and replied to it in a few careless phrases. But it seemed to him that her silence was golden, as golden as the gleams in her changeful hazel eyes as the sun smote on them.

'If you would allow me to go,' she murmured, 'I have quite enough flowers here. It is such a small church, and the orchids would be much too rare——'

'If the orchids were made of rubies and pearls, what happier fate could they ask than to fall from your hands on to the altars of the Madonna?' said Othmar, as he broke off the blossoms of his camellias with no sparing hand.

At that moment the head-gardener, alarmed and disturbed at the message which he had received from his master, came in sight with a basket hurriedly filled with some of the choicest treasures of his forcing-houses.

Othmar took it from him:

'You did quite right,' he said in a low tone, 'to make my friends welcome to the gardens in my absence, but another time, M. Duvelleroy, make them welcome to the best; do not reserve it for the markets and the florist shops of Nice.'

The man, guilty, and taken at a disadvantage, had no time to prepare a lie; he grew red, and stammered, and was thankful for his master's gesture of dismissal as Othmar turned from him impatiently and offered the orchids to the girl.

'You are angry with him,' she said, anxiety conquering her timidity.

'Not so; I am grateful to him,' said Othmar. 'But I shall, perhaps, be angry with my house-steward, whose duty it is to keep these rogues clean-handed. If he had given you his best flowers I would have pensioned him for life, but to limit you to taking what he did not want to sell, was to disgrace S. Pharamond.'

'Indeed, he has been very kind all these three winters,' she murmured, in infinite distress at the thought that she had inadvertently injured the man in his master's opinion.

'He shall wear the order of St. Fiacre if you like, if there be such an order to reward good gardeners,' said Othmar gaily, seeing her genuine anxiety on the man's behalf. 'I may come and see your decorations to-morrow. Shall I send you a load of flowers? That would be better I think.'

She looked alarmed.

'Oh no; oh pray, do not!' she said with earnestness. 'You are very kind to think of it, Monsieur, but it would frighten the curé, and we should not know what to do with so many, the church is so very small——'

She hesitated a moment, the colour in her cheeks grew warm as she added:

'My cousin does not know that I come here. I do not mean that it is any secret, but she might think it wrong, intrusive, impertinent——'

'She could think nothing of the sort,' said Othmar. 'They are three words which no one could associate with Mdlle. de Valogne; I am delighted my deserted house could be so honoured. Must you go? I shall not easily forgive myself if I frighten you away. Let me come with you to the gate at least.'

He walked beside her under the palms and on the shaven grass down an aisle of clipped arbutus, carrying for her the camellias, white and rose, which he had broken off their plants with no care for the appearance of the group to which they belonged.

She was silent; she was subdued by an unwonted sense of wrong-doing; she fancied that she had committed some terrible indiscretion; but how was she to have known that he was there, when for three winters the camellias had blossomed unseen in those silent evergreen ways, which no step but a gardener's had ever disturbed, and where she had come to watch the blackbirds trip over the fallen leaves, and the fountains dance in the sunshine, and the tea-roses shower petals of cream and of gold on the terraces, with no more thought or hesitation than she had gone to the olive-yards of Nicole Sandros? Her confusion had nothing of awkwardness. It was very graceful, almost stately, in its silence; it was the grave innocence, the startled hesitation, of the young nymph surprised in the sanctuary of the grove.

She accepted the orchids with a serious gratitude, which seemed to him quite out of proportion to the slenderness of the gift; but when he said as much she interrupted him:

'They are so beautiful,' she said earnestly. 'It seems cruel to have plucked them. One fancies they will take wing like the butterflies.'

'You are very fond of flowers?'

'Oh yes—and people waste them so. At my cousin's ball last week there were five thousand roses. I saw them in the morning; they were quite dead.'

'Did you not see them at night?'

'At night, no; how could I? I am not in the world; I never shall be. Sometimes they tell me to be an hour in the reception-rooms after dinner; that is all; I do not care for it.'

'But do you not wish for the time of balls to come? Every young girl does.'

'I try never to think about it,' she said simply. 'I know it will never come for me.'

There was a resignation in her words which was more pathetic than any regrets.

Then with the colour hot in her cheeks again, remembering that she was speaking too much to a stranger, she opened the little gate in the arbutus walk which led into the grounds of Millo. 'I thank you very much,' she murmured. 'I assure you I will never come again.'

'And unless you come again, I assure you that you will tell me tacitly that I have had the misfortune to displease you,' said Othmar, as he held open the gate, and bowed low to her; he saw that it would be only unkindness to detain her or to accompany her. She was as uneasy as a bird which has flown by mistake into a conservatory.

'I will come to the church to-morrow,' he added. 'Do you not sing there sometimes?'

'Now and then. There is no one else to sing. But my cousin does not approve of it. She thinks there may be people over from Nice; but there never are. There is no one but the peasants.'

'The Duchesse will not mind me,' said Othmar. 'Let us say *au revoir*!'

He kissed her hand with a careless gallantry which made her colour over her brow and throat, and let her leave him. She sped like a frightened fawn over the turf and was soon lost to sight in the bosquets of Millo.

Othmar strolled back to the house.

'Au tombeau seul finit ma voie obscure,'

he repeated to himself as he looked after her; the pathos of her destiny gave her a spirituality and a sanctity in his sight, and the song of the blind child and its young singer for a few moments disputed a place in his memory with the vision of Nadine Napraxine as she had plucked the tea-roses on his terrace to let them fall.

'That young girl would not let a rose fade,' he thought, 'and her own roses are to wither between convent walls! What arbitrary caprices has Fate! If they would only let me give her a million——'

But they would not even have let him give her orchids and camellias had they known it.

---

# CHAPTER IX.

Othmar went into his house, but before taking his coffee sent for his steward, and gave him a brief but severe reprimand for having permitted Duvelleroy and his underlings to use the gardens as a nursery-ground.

'The grounds may be sacked to please my friends,' he said, in conclusion. 'But if a single carnation be sold for a single centime, it is not the seller who will be dismissed, but yourself, who are paid highly only that you may save your subordinates from those temptations which kill honesty and should be no more left in the path of poor men than poisoned mangolds in a sheep-field.'

The notion that his hothouses and gardens had furnished the flower-sellers of Nice with materials for their myriads of bouquets, irritated him disproportionately. He would have taken his oath that on none of his estates did his people steal a farthing's worth. They were all highly paid, and those set in authority over them were all men who had been chosen and enriched by his father; he had often spoken of their probity and affection with pride; and now they cheated him for sake of selling a bouquet!

It was a mere trifle, no doubt. He would have cleared his gardens at a stroke to please anyone he liked; and he would have given a poor man willingly the value of all his forcing houses; but the knowledge that his hirelings sold his mignonette and his heliotrope to profit themselves irritated him, and even quite embittered life to him for the moment. The most generous minds feel the most acutely betrayal in small things, and resent most vividly the contemptible robberies which take advantage of trust and opportunity. That the rich man is so seldom honestly served goes further, perhaps, to redress the balance between him and the poor man than the latter, in his ignorance, ever supposes.

'After all,' he thought, 'perhaps I only feed rogues, like Napraxine.' And the thought was painful to him, for he fed them well.

It was primarily his own fault for so seldom coming to the place; perhaps it was natural that when years rolled on and they never saw their master they should learn to consider his possessions as almost their own. But he had so many places that he could not live in them all. His fathers had bought them, so, out of respect to their memories, he could not get rid of them. He had a great house on the Boulevard St. Germain; another great house in Piccadilly; another in the Teresian Platz of Vienna; he had estates in France, England, Germany, and Austria, a Scotch moor, a Flemish forest, a château on the shores of the Dalmatian Adriatic, a villa at Biarritz, a castle in dense woods on the Moselle, and whole towns, villages, plains, and hills in Croatia itself. How was he to live at all these places? He lent them liberally, but he could hardly sell them; the head of the house of Othmar could not sell what he had inherited. If he had sold them he would only have had more millions with which he would not have known what to do.

When he had drunk a cup of coffee and a glass of iced water, he went for a long ride, mounting high up into the hills until the sea lay far below, blue as a great bed of mysotis, and the gilded cupolas of La Jacquemerille glittered in his sight far beneath the darkening slopes of pine. When he returned to his one o'clock breakfast, he found that his house was deserted no more. He was told that his uncle, the Baron Friederich, had arrived by the *rapide* from Paris. He was not greatly pleased, but he prepared to do his duties as a host without betraying his sense that the new comer was not precisely in harmony with a romantic retreat amidst myrtles, camellias, and bromelias.

But he also foresaw a tedious day and evening, and he did not care to have the keen blue eyes of his father's brother fixed on him at a moment when he was sending telegrams in all directions and commanding all kinds of novel diversions to amuse and receive the Princess Napraxine.

'Have your travels tended to convince you that Europeans are wrong not to let the tails of sheep fatten and appear at their tables?' said his unbidden guest, coming out of the house as though they had parted the previous night instead of twenty months before.

There was no figure better known in Paris than that of the Baron Friederich Othmar, familiar to society all over Europe as Baron Fritz; a tall and portly figure carried with the ease and vigour of manhood, though age had whitened the hair, that was still abundant, on the handsome head above. He never attempted to conceal his age: he despised all *maquillage*, as all healthy and all clever men do; and if his skin was as fair and his hands were as white and soft as a duchess's, it was because nature had made them so, and a life temperate in indulgence though entirely unscrupulous in morals had preserved his health and his strength unimpaired save by occasional twinges of the gout. With old Gaulois blood in him, Friederich Othmar was a thorough Parisian in habit, taste, and manner; but he was a true Slav in suppleness, sagacity, and profound secretiveness. Othmar thought that there was not on the face of the earth another man with such a hideous power of dissimulation as his uncle; whilst the elder man, on the contrary, looked upon such dissimulation as the mere mark which distinguishes the civilised being from the savage. 'Dissimulation lies at the root of all good manners,' he was wont to say in moments of frankness. 'Your friend bores you infinitely; you smile, and appear charmed! If you do not, you are a boor. Dissimulation is the essence of Christianity; you are enjoined to turn one cheek after another, and not to show that you smart. Dissimulation is the only thing that makes society possible; without its amenities, the world would be a bear-garden.'

On the Bourse 'Baron Fritz' was dreaded as the keenest-witted colossus of finance in all Europe. His acumen was unerring; his mind was as sensitive to the changes of the political atmosphere as an electric wire to heat. He perceived long before anyone else the little cloud, not so big as a man's hand, which was pregnant with storm whilst yet the sky was clear; he heard long before anyone else the low tremor in the bowels of the earth which prefaced the seismic convulsion, as yet undreamed of by a sleeping world. Therefore, with supreme tact and matchless instinct, he had made the House of Othmar the envy of all its peers. 'What are statesmen without us?' said Friederich Othmar. 'They cannot move, they cannot strike, unless the financiers enable them to do so; all their combinations crumble like a dropt bird's-nest unless we are willing to sustain them. If Germany had had no money, could she have crossed the Rhine? The finest army in the world is no more than a child's set of metal soldiers if it be not *roulant sur l'or*. The statesmen are thought to be the chief rulers and prime motors of the fate of the world, but they can but act as we who are behind them permit: they drag the coach; we drive it.'

'That I know,' answered Othmar. 'We have the most gigantic responsibility united with the most utterly corrupt moral code. I grant that we are, in a way, the Cæsars of the modern world, but we are bestially selfish; we are hog-like in our repletion, as all Cæsars become. No financier ever risked ruin for a noble impulse or for a lost cause. If he did, he would seem mad to his guild, as Ulysses to his companions.'

All the enjoyment and sense of power which Othmar contemptuously rejected his uncle appreciated to the full; he was, in his own way, a Wolsey, a Richelieu, a Bismarck. Nothing of much importance had been done in Europe for the last forty years without Friederich Othmar being beneath it, in more or less degree, for weal or woe. He had those unerring instincts which amount in their own way to genius.

Endowed with one of those keen, logical, yet imaginative brains, which are as necessary to the great financier as to the great statesman, he had worked unweariedly all his life long for the sake and for the glory of the house of Othmar; he was in no way of his nephew's opinion; he considered that the world held nothing finer than the fortunes which had been built up out of Marc Othmar's kreutzers till it was solid as so many towers of bullion; he considered the position of the capitalist who can refuse a king, sustain a nation, fructify great enterprises, and constrain or restrain great wars, was not to be exchanged with any other power under the sun. In finance he was inexorable, unerring; full of the finest penetration, and the most piercing acumen; stern as granite, piercing as steel; in private life he was an amiable cynic, who cared for very little except the reputation of his dinners and his collection of water-colours. Baron Fritz was never really content out of his little hotel, which was as cosy as a satin-lined bag, and where by stretching out a finger to touch an ivory button he could put himself in communication with all the centres of finance in Europe. Without moving from his velvet chair or taking his foot from its gout-stool he could converse with his brother capitalists at all quarters of the globe, and change the fate of nations, and the surface of events in the course of a winter's forenoon during a pause between two cigarettes. To be able to do so seemed to him the very flower and perfection of life. It was to play chess with the world for your board, and to say checkmate to living and crowned kings.

Whenever he expatiated on that theme to his nephew, Othmar only replied that he himself did not care for any games.

For the rest, his one great social amusement was whist; he could never see why men forsook their clubs because hay was being mown and corn reaped and grapes gathered. You bought forage, you ate bread—very little of it—and you drank wine, but why, because those three things were all in their embryo state every city in Europe should become empty he had not patience to comprehend. No place was cooler, shadier, quieter, than your club. The vast green silent country which his nephew loved was to him an outer darkness; he detested *le province* with all the maliciousness against it of a born and bred Parisian.

To see a breezy common on a six-inch square of David Cox, or a brook purling amongst rushes by Bonnington, was to have as much of the country as he cared to enjoy. The stones of Vienna, the asphalte of Paris, were the only ground he cared to tread. He had educated his cook into perfect excellence, and never travelled anywhere without him and his battery of silver saucepans. 'Because you sleep in a strange bed there is no reason why you should let yourself be poisoned by strange dishes,' he invariably said.

On the whole he had led a happy and enviable life; he was a perfectly selfish man, with one great unselfish loyalty set in the midst of his egotism, like a vein of pure marble amongst a mass of sandstone. 'To benefit the House Fritz would let himself be brayed in a mortar,' his brother had often said of him; in private life, on the contrary, he was entirely self-absorbed, as became a man who was one of the most notable persons in Paris; he had never been known to lend a five-franc piece, but he gave choice dinners three times a week, which cost twenty napoleons for each guest.

Sometimes he thought with a pang of terror of what would become of the House of Othmar when he himself should be no more. He was seventy years old; he would be unable to live for ever; his arsenal of wires contained no ivory button by which he could summon eternal life; he had gout in his system, and he did not disguise from himself that any day his cook, with the silver saucepans, his pretty aquarelles, his gigantic operations, his intense love of life, might one and all be powerless to keep him in his place, and then!—all the magnitude and might of the House of Othmar would depend solely and entirely on one capricious and unstable young man, who only cared for a Greek poet or a German opera!

On these melancholy days when he remembered this, he voluntarily deprived himself of his burgundy, and ate only of two dishes.

He was much attached to Othmar, but he was impatient of him. He was annoyed by what he looked upon as his crotchets and caprices; he was irritated by the unconcealed apathy and even scorn with which his nephew regarded his own superb position in the world. The dissatisfaction with which the origin of their House filled the head of it, was to Baron Fritz almost incomprehensible and whimsical squeamishness. If he revered anything in life, it was the tradition of old Marc Othmar amassing his florins in the half-barbaric city of Agram.

'For aught we know he was a Tchigan, a Romany,' his nephew had said to him once; and he had replied angrily, 'And if he were a gipsy? Is there blood more ancient? Is there a people freer? Is there an intelligence more complex? What are the European races beside the Oriental? But you know very well that he was a pure Croat,' he had concluded, with intolerable impatience of such depreciation of the founder of their greatness.

Although it had been the habit of his life to follow and study the minds of men even in their more secret thoughts, he had no patience to attempt to understand the caprices of his nephew's. It was, he thought, that kind of ingratitude to fate which is almost an insanity; the same sort of fractious wilfulness which made James of Scotland love to wander disguised in his own towns, and sent Domitian to a plot of cabbages.

To Baron Fritz the power and might of the House he belonged to had ever been in the stead of any other religion, creed, or attachment; he was not personally an ambitious or an avaricious man; he had effaced himself for his brother's sake, as he still slaved for his brother's son; the celebrity of the House of Othmar, their power, heavy as an elephant's tread, subtle as an electric current, the magnitude of the operations which they either undertook or impeded, the respect with which Europe regarded them, the weight of their own smile or frown,—all these things were the very breath of his life to him. He had remained, and always willingly remained, a subordinate; he had never resented the superiority of his elder brother in power and position; all he had cared to do was to give his years to the service and aggrandisement of his race; he would have been very astonished if he had been told that it was in its way, after all, chiefly a form of sentiment which actuated him.

Between himself and Othmar there was the affection of consanguinity, but no sympathy whatever. To the elder man the younger seemed almost blasphemously unworthy of his heritage: the generosities and the scruples of such a *raffiné* seemed to him the perverseness of a child. Usually, Othmar willingly abandoned to him the guidance of their great argosy, freighted with the gold of the world, but twice or thrice since his majority he had interfered when he had considered a loan immoral or an enterprise corrupt, and had made his veto, as head of the house, obeyed forcibly. Those few times had been unpardonable to the Baron who had not his eccentric and quixotic principles.

'Affairs are affairs,' he said. 'If you conduct them according to the follies and phantasies of the Story of Arthur—adieu.'

'I would willingly say adieu—an eternal adieu,' had retorted Othmar. 'But you have told me repeatedly that I cannot withdraw my House from business without causing ruin on the Bourses of Europe, and dishonouring our name by annulling and repudiating our engagements.'

'Of course you cannot,' had said the Baron, to whom the mere idea seemed like a preparation to blow up with dynamite all the mountains of Europe and of Asia. 'Do you suppose you can efface such an institution as our financial existence? You might as well say that a sovereign, by dying, could will his country into non-existence.'

'Then as I cannot touch the engagements of the past, however much I condemn them, I will at least keep pure the obligations of the future,' Othmar had answered; and those transactions which his more delicate sense of honour did not allow him to approve he refused to permit to be undertaken.

Baron Fritz, who had the ordinary financier's conscience, that is, who would have done nothing commercially dishonourable, but who cared not a straw how iniquitous might be the results of an operation, so long as it was legal, clever, and lucrative, was beyond measure irritated by this occasional interference of one who was too fine a gentleman, too indolent a dreamer, to bear any of the frets and burden of habitual attention to their gigantic operations. But there was no help for it; Otho Othmar was the head of the House, and, what was a greater grief still to his uncle, the only living one of the name besides himself. They, who could have given fortunes and position to a score of younger branches, who could have had their sons and brothers objects of power and worship in all the capitals of Europe, had been so visited by death and destiny that of them all there only remained the young man who was Othmar to all the world, and the old one who was Baron Fritz to his intimate associates, and Baron Friederich to all the Bourses.

'You should marry, Otho,' said the Baron to him now.

'I have no inclination to do so,' he answered, and thought of Nadine Napraxine.

'Inclination!' exclaimed the other irritably. 'What has inclination to do with it? Is inclination considered or waited for in the marriages of princes? You are a prince in your own way. If you died to-morrow, your race would be extinct.'

'That would not much matter,' said Othmar. 'We have never been conspicuous for anything except for amassing gold, as a ship's keel collects barnacles. I suppose I had better make a will. You shall have everything for your lifetime, and then it shall all go to the French Republic, which is the only national institution I know of that is capable of muddling away two hundred milliards in a year, with nothing whatever to show for it afterwards.'

Baron Fritz made a gesture of irritated contempt.

'You ought to have had legitimate heirs ten years ago. You do not belong to yourself. You have no right to live and die without raising up posterity.'

'I do not see the obligation,' said Othmar, 'and I do not care enough about the name, which you think so very fine, to greatly grieve over its probable extinction.'

Baron Fritz had heard this often, but he never heard it freshly without an inward shudder, such as a religious man feels before a blasphemy. Othmar, merely as a man, seemed to him a fanciful dreamer, an unsatisfactory anomaly, an unphilosophic thinker, whose theories were always playing the deuce with his interest, and whose sympathies ran away with him like half-broken horses. But Othmar, as the chief of his House, could do no wrong, and had to be obeyed, even if he rushed on his own destruction.

'You should marry for sake of posterity,' he reiterated. 'You are so happily and exceptionally situated that you can choose wherever you please. No living woman would refuse you. You should seek physical charms for sake of your offspring and high lineage also; the rest is a mere matter of taste.'

'The rest is only a trifle! Only character, mind, and feeling—the three things which determine happiness and influence life more than anything else.'

Baron Fritz made a little gesture of indifference: 'I imagine anyone *bien élevé* would not err in any of these points. Happiness one usually finds with the wives of others. Not that I would discourage you if you be inclined——'

'I am not inclined,' said Othmar, brusquely. 'I only say that character is never considered by men and women when they marry; yet it is what makes or mars a life. When a marriage is announced, what is discussed? The respective fortunes of those concerned, then their good looks or their lack of them; perhaps someone adds that he is *bon garçon*, or someone says *sa taille est jolie*, or, on the other hand, they may say he is a fool, or she has ugly feet; but you never hear a word as to their characters, their sympathies, or their principles. It is why all marriages are at best but a compromise between two ill-assorted dispositions.'

'Make yours well-assorted,' said Baron Fritz. 'If you attach so much to character, let character be your study; myself, I have always considered that marriage is a means of continuing a race, so that it legally can continue to transmit property; I have never known why people imported fine sentiments into a legal transaction. It is taking a false view of a social duty to look for personal pleasure out of it; indeed, if a man be in love with his wife he will probably communicate his passion to her, which is undesirable, because it awakens her senses, and ultimately leads to her taking a lover, or lovers, which again introduces uncertainty into the legal enjoyment and transmission of property.'

Othmar smiled: 'Really, Baron, you are the most profoundly immoral man I ever met. You would always, too, subordinate humanity to property. All human actions should, according to you, only tend to the consolidation and concentration of fortune; now, there is no possible theory of human action more demoralising.'

'That is a matter of opinion,' said the Baron. 'But unless your forefathers had carried that theory into practice, you would now be taming wild horses in Croatia, or probably you—Otho Othmar in your entity as you are— would not exist at all, for certainly your father would not have wedded with an English aristocrat.'

'It is a humiliating reflection,' said Othmar, 'that one's existence depended on the accidental union of two persons; indeed, I decline to believe it. I am convinced that the real *ego*, the impersonal entity which has been called the soul for want of knowing what to call it, must have had its own independent existence; the envelope it is slipped into is the accident; let us think so at all events. It is more consoling than your notion that the entire life of A. depended on the chance of B. cohabiting with C.; and that if B. had wedded D. instead, A. would never have existed at all, but another and totally different being would have done so—say Z.'

The Baron shrugged his shoulders. Why, he wondered, why on earth should a man care about a pre-existence, or a spiritual existence, at all, who had everything that his heart could desire in his terrestrial life? He could imagine that starving poets or hungry theologians comforted themselves with those fancies, but Othmar!——

'You should have been a Montalembert or a Lamennais,' he answered, which was a polite way of saying that he was an imbecile.

'Without being either the one or the other, one may carry into public life the same sort of honour which even you think incumbent on one in public life,' said Othmar.

'Not at all,' said his relative. 'The code for one has never been the code for the other. A man in private life may not send another man to be slain because it suits his purpose; a man in public life, that is, as a war minister or as an officer commanding-in-chief may send ten thousand, fifty thousand, men to certain slaughter. So has a diplomatist every title to lie as much as he may need to do in the public service, but he has no right to deceive his personal friend in a private matter. This is not mere casuistry; it is common-sense. Indeed, all effective casuistry is based on common-sense.'

'The most dangerous casuistry is so, no doubt,' said Othmar. 'Because when it is so based it is irresistible in its appeal to egotism.'

'I do not know why you use the word dangerous,' replied the Baron. 'Nothing is so wholesome as to teach men to take care of their own interests. If that lesson were universally understood, there would be neither paupers or criminals.'

'We should have a world of bankers,' said Othmar. 'With all deference to you, even that would not be a Millennium.'

The Baron assented with good humour that it would certainly not be one, since there would be no investments of any kind possible.

The day was tedious to Othmar. He had to examine many projects, and append his signature to many documents. He had not disappeared into Central Asia for eighteen months without having brought upon himself the penalty of many arrears of affairs. His assent was merely *pro formâ*, but the formula was necessary.

'He is in love still with Madame Napraxine,' thought his uncle, finding his attention hard to fix. He was not sorry for that. At Othmar's age he was sure to be in love with someone, and the more he was in love the less likely was he to meddle with the transactions of the House.

The Baron could be excessively amusing, and was so this day of his arrival at S. Pharamond; but Othmar would gladly have been free of his presence. He knew that the old man would see at a glance, if he and Nadine Napraxine met before him, that time had not cured him of passion; and the malice and the contempt of his uncle were both disagreeable to him. Moreover, Othmar had been too perpetually agreed with all his life to be pleased by the constant enunciation of opinions and sentiments the reverse of his own. There was that in the tranquil cynicism of Baron Friederich which left him with a sense of moral nausea. Men, it is true, were not worth much; but he could never get accustomed to the calm manner in which his uncle was habitually ready to sacrifice all their interests—their bodies, too, had there been any question of them—to what he considered advantageous to himself and to his house in public life and finance.

He did not care for the new Russian loan, for the new Turkish loan, for the great naval dockyards to be made by Germany on the Baltic, for the railway that was to be driven along the ancient bed of the Oxus, nor for the necessities of the empire of Brazil, nor for the development of Canadian forests. It did not interest him that such and such a sovereign would be a cripple without his help, or such and such a country as virtually in pawn to him as though it had been a pledged estate; that the assistance of his gold could enable a Ministry to keep its tenure of office, or the refusal of it could precipitate a State into revolution; to Baron Fritz it was like holding the reins of the universe, but to Othmar himself it was excessively dull work. The heir of four generations of money-lenders, he was absolutely indifferent to the immense power which lay in the stroke of his pen; the genius of finance was inherited by him, though dormant in him; even his uncle did justice to the accuracy of his vision, to the certainty of his instinct; but it was genius unused; he had no taste to employ its capacities. Europe was as indifferent to him as a mound of clay.

'We only do mischief, unmitigated mischief,' he asserted very often. 'Look at the Canal of Suez; it has only bred wars and pretexts for wars, and will probably embroil England and France for the next century,—until indeed India shall have become Russian, or the African negro have avenged Abd-el-Kadir. Then again take the Panama project: it will set Great Britain and the United States at each other's throats like two bull-dogs.'

'You are enough to make your father rise from his grave,' said Baron Fritz.

'It is only aristocrats who do that,' returned Othmar. 'The financier sleeps sound on the remembrance of his own virtues—and loans.'

The memory of his father was bitter to him; he could not forget the injury done to him in his earliest youth by subjecting him to the charms and the corruptions of Sara Vernon.

'You must marry, and then you will see things differently,' his uncle insisted, reverting to the simplicity of reiteration.

What a cruel thing was destiny! Thousands of men who had not a crust of bread begat legitimate offsprings in the most reckless and profuse manner; and the one man for whom lawful heirs were an absolute necessity and duty obstinately neglected his obligations to family and to the world.

It was possible, even probable, that the last of the Othmars would remain the last of his race.

'Marry for me,' said Othmar. 'I will give all we possess to any cousins you may give me, and keep only enough myself to live peaceably in Arabia Felix. I have always wished to live there; the climate is divine; and, after all, there is nothing that is of so much consequence as climate.'

'You will always jest!'

'Most people say I am too serious. I am not jesting at all. We have all a sort of superstition that we must live in Europe, but it is only a superstition. There is a great deal finer weather elsewhere, and without fine weather life is intolerable.'

'Have you never seen a woman you would marry?' asked Baron Fritz.

'Perhaps I have,' said Othmar, who never lied. 'But never one I could marry.'

'Ah!—someone else's wife! That is just like you. If she were not unattainable she would have no more attraction than anyone else. You are so whimsical.'

'I hope not. I dislike whimsical people. They are always asking for the windows to be shut, or imagining that there is a drainpipe open. Oh, some day I may marry. I do not pledge my future. But I have no inclination to marriage, and you will confess that you preach what you do not practise.'

'I am seventy-one and you are thirty-two,' said Baron Fritz; 'I should have married fifty years ago if I had been as you are, the head of the House.'

'Curse the House!' said Othmar, though he was a man who never used any oaths, great or small. But it seemed to him that the House of Othmar was for ever on his shoulders like Sindbad's burden; that he could do nothing freely as other men did; that go where he would he could never wholly escape from the mephitic acid which adulation and importunity exhale, and could never gain that simplicity of existence which, precisely because it was denied to him, seemed to him the chief good on earth.

'You speak as if the Othmars had been Plantagenets or Comneni!' he continued. 'It is not quite two centuries ago that the world did not even know that a Croat horse-dealer bore that name! The last time I was at Agram, I looked into the archives of the city; nobody ever did so; they were crabbed and hard to decipher; but I passed a day over them when it was raining and blowing so hard that there was not a soul abroad in the streets except the sentries. In the municipal documents for the year 1730 I found an account of a famine which had been the result of floods such as we have seen in our own day, for science, after all, makes little way against natural catastrophes. It was during this famine, when every grain of wheat was worth treble its weight in gold, that your hero Marc Othmar made his first great *coup*. He had amassed money before, but this was the grand conception which first largely enriched him. He had bought enormously in corn, foreseeing a wet season and bad harvests. He had more than he had hoped for—he had the whole country under water. He had almost a monopoly of grain. In those days government aid could not come by steam, and besides, Croatia had just then no government. In these records it is stated that upwards of forty-five thousand persons, chiefly women and children, died of starvation; and all the while they were dying Marc Othmar shut up his grain and only sold it sack by sack, at an average rate of a death a bushel. You find that admirable; I do not. I confess, ever since I put these facts together out of the fragments of public history, it has seemed to me as if there were an earthy smell about all our money; you know the lungs of people who die starved always do smell like decaying mould. It is pure fancy—I am quite aware of that. But even, putting fancy out of the question, I do not see anything heroic about the figure of our founder. He is not Hugh Lupus or Godfrey de Bouillon.'

Baron Fritz's patience had scarcely endured the strain upon it.

'I never heard the story. I believe you have invented it,' he said irritably. 'If it be true, we have no explanation, so we cannot form a correct judgment. At the most, accepting it as you relate it, no more was done then by Marc Othmar than every farmer or peasant proprietor in Europe and America does whenever he gets a chance. Not so much as was done by Ferdinand de Lesseps when he sacrificed the fellahs to make his Egyptian Canal. You cannot conduct any trade on abstract principles or æsthetic moralities. You must buy cheap and sell dear, or commerce falls to the ground, and the whole superstructure of society falls with it. As the lawyer cannot refuse to conduct a case because he disapproves of the morality of it, so a financier cannot let pass a favourable operation because he may not approve entirely of its scope; all he has to examine are its wisdom and utility. When once you enter the region of motives and of principles, all is confusion. No two men have the same views as to what is right; you must proceed on broader lines than those of fanciful ethics. For instance, nothing is more clearly immoral than the marriage of two diseased persons, but the priest or the mayor who should refuse to perform the ceremonies demanded of him because he conceived that the bodily health of the people came before him was unsatisfactory would be clearly overpassing the boundaries of his functions, which are limited to the consideration of simply legal obstacles. So, a man of business who once concerns himself with the vague moralities of his speculations is lost; all he has to occupy himself with is their solvency, their legality, and their probabilities of success or failure. Marc Othmar, no doubt, regarded his investments in corn in that purely practical light.'

'For a very clever man as you are,' returned Othmar, 'you are curiously unconscious of what a satire your theories are on all that you most admire. I am as entirely convinced as you can be that Marc Othmar never gave a thought to the twenty-five thousand people who starved to death while his corn was shut up in granaries and barges; all the difference between us is, that you think this singleness of eye for his own interest was heroic, and I think it was not so,—that it was even as near true hellish wickedness as humanity can go.'

'There is neither wickedness nor virtue in questions of finance,' said Baron Friederich, with distress at his nephew's obtuseness.

'There is certainly no virtue,' said Othmar.

'Neither wickedness nor virtue,' repeated the Baron. 'They are pure abstractions, like political economy. To talk of the immorality of a speculation is like talking of the vices of a rock-crystal. There is only one sin in a financial operation; it sins if it be unsound.'

'Financial morality,' then said Othmar, 'has at least this advantage over social morality, that it is very much simplified!'

'It is simple as your stable's doctrines,' replied the Baron. 'If a horse be sound, he is a good horse; if he be not sound, he is a screw; nothing can be simpler. And the moment that a man begins to confuse himself with asking any more complex questions than this one, "Is it sound?"—whether he engage in a great operation of finance, or whether he be only buying a roadster, he will be inevitably bewildered with his own multiform requirements and will fall into the hands of mere persuasive sharpers.'

'I can buy a horse,' said Othmar, 'but I will leave finance to you.'

'Not always,' said Baron Fritz, grimly, with vivid recollections of more than one occasion on which his nephew had interfered with a peremptory veto to prevent some contemplated operation of which the morality was more doubtful than the expediency. The occasions had been rare indeed; but they had left an ineffaceable soreness on the mind of the elder man; nay, he would scarcely have forgiven them had it not been that his devotion to Otho as to the head of the House had something of the irrational and patient loyalty which the Russian nation renders blindly to its unseen Tzar.

As for Othmar himself, he was too impatient of his uncle's laxity of principle and conscience to do full justice to the fine qualities which accompanied these.

Those huge stone palaces whose portals bore the magic name of Othmar were sacred to Baron Fritz as his temples to a Greek. His nephew never passed through the great doors of any one of them without a sense of impatience, of distaste, without a remembrance of the twenty-five thousand people who had died of hunger in Croatia whilst Marc Othmar was building up his piles of ducats and florins. The very homage with which he was himself met within their walls irritated him. He thought of all the debasing worship the earth has seen the worship of riches was the most corrupt. 'If I were a leper they would kiss my ulcers so long as my hand could sign a cheque,' he thought. After all, when Marc Othmar had used up human lives in the furnace of his speculations he had used up material which was but of little worth.

Yet despite the disdain which human nature cannot do otherwise than awaken in those who are the objects of its adulation if they keep their senses clear amidst the incense fumes, his heart was empty.

'You have people here to-night?' asked the Baron, a little later, his vigilant eyes perceiving the preparations which were being made in the little theatre attached to the château.

'To-morrow night,' answered Othmar. 'A small dinner; I hope you will remain for it. And as Talazac, Sembrich, and other good singers are at Nice *disponibles*, we shall have some music afterwards and a few people; for that you will not care.'

'The Napraxines are here?' enquired his uncle, with a little smile.

Othmar was annoyed to feel that he changed colour despite himself, as he answered in the affirmative.

'Have you seen her?' said Friederich Othmar, carelessly. 'How do you find her? *Maladive* as usual?'

'There is no woman living less *maladive*,' said Othmar, with some irritation. 'She is glad to make the care of her health a pretext when she is disinclined for the world; that is all.'

'Ah, indeed?' said the elder man. 'All great rulers are allowed to be ill at their own convenience. Will she be ill or well to-morrow night?'

'Time will show,' replied Othmar, in a tone which closed the subject.

---

# CHAPTER X.

It was a tiny church which bore the name of S. Cecilia at S. Pharamond, and was perched on an olive-covered knoll, with the rolling woods of the château d'Othmar at its base and the gardens of Millo on its right. Nicole Sandroz and a few other families of the *petite culture* gathered there on Sundays and holy days; but the great people of Millo, with their household, had their own private chapel, and the friends to whom Othmar had lent his house had never troubled themselves to find their way to the little whitewashed, wind-blown sanctuary and the lowly presbytery that leaned up against its south wall.

Othmar himself, who had a score of ecclesiastics in a score of places looking to him for support, had hardly known that this little church and its old purblind peasant-born curé were upon the confines of his estate. He had paid every year a large sum for the maintenance of S. Pharamond, as for that of each of his houses and estates, but he had never examined the details of the expenditure. The advantage of an immense fortune is that you can leave all such matters to your secretaries. He paid them more heed than many would have done because of the views he entertained on the duties of saving other people from temptation; but S. Pharamond, with all its luxuries, elegancies, gardens, carriages, and conservatories, was only to him as a mere cottage, a mere toy. He had, indeed, almost forgotten that he had owned it, until, beating up the Bay of Genoa in a storm-tossed and almost disabled vessel, he had suddenly remembered that somewhere on this coast which slid away in the dusk to the westward he had a harbour and a quay all his own if he chose to go thither.

The little church was ugly, poor, and had been built since the Revolution; all that redeemed it was a great climbing rose which covered the whole of its front, and was even flinging audacious branches upwards to the cross upon the roof. In summer the rose made the little plain square place a glory of pink bloom. Inside, there were a few deal benches, a few bad prints, a humble little altar, and some pewter candlesticks; the presbytery was equally as bare.

The old vicar lived with one servant as old as himself; he toddled out amongst the farms, and was scouted and scowled at by some of the peasants, petted and welcomed by others. He did no harm, and was quite happy if one of his parishioners gave him a basket of figs or a dish of seakale; he could almost have counted his flock on his fingers. The men about there were very radical and hard-headed; they were all small proprietors, who cursed Millo and S. Pharamond all the year round, though neither the villa nor the château did them the slightest harm. On the contrary, the stewards of both the Duc de Vannes and Othmar had orders to give away any rare seeds, aid in any irrigation-works, or contribute to any need that there might be in the neighbourhood. But the Duc was a duke and peer of France, and Othmar was an archimillionaire; the *petite culture* hated the sight of their gilded bronze gates and their glittering high-pitched roofs.

'It is for you that we pay taxes!' snarled one of them once to the Duc de Vannes, who laughed and answered:

'Oh, my friend, if we compared notes I think you would find that it is I who pay them for you and yours. I have not the slightest objection to do so, only do not let us misrepresent matters.'

But they did not want logic, and they hated the steep shining roofs and the gates with the gilded scroll work. What they did not hate was Yseulte de Valogne; all countess though she was, they pardoned her that defect because she had always remained for them *la pétiote de Nicole*. They understood that she was to be sacrificed to the pride of her relatives; that because she was poor, so poor, she was to be refused all the joys of her youth and her sex and surrendered to the Church that she might not offend the grandeur of her family by making a portionless marriage. This, which they had learned, with many exaggerations of its enormity from Nicole and from the servants of Millo, gave her the halo of a martyr in their eyes; she was sacrificed to the *noblesse*, and that fact was enough to make her sacred to them even though she belonged to the detested order herself, and had not a little of its hauteur. Besides, her tenderness to their old people, the little gifts she made at the convent and brought to their little ones and their women, her intrepidity in cases of sickness in those winters when she was alone at Millo—a mere child, but with the courage of giants, as Nicole loved to tell—all these, joined to her personal elegance, which made her as unlike themselves as the orchids in Othmar hothouses were unlike the sweet peas and the lavender growing under their peach trees, had combined to make of the last Comtesse de Valogne the idol of *petite culture* which, with few exceptions, loathed and execrated the brilliant idlers who rode and drove out of the gates of Millo, and carried their light laughter, their painted fans, their blazing jewels, their grace and their luxuries, out on to the illuminated terraces, under the palms and the araucarias, amidst the lamps and the music, regardless of the people in the distant huts and houses on the surrounding hills who, rising to their work, as they went to their beds, swore savagely against them with all the unchanged rancorous class-hatred of the Terror still alive in them and unsatisfied.

'But, Nicole,' the girl said often to her foster-mother, 'if there were no rich people, no great people, who would buy your *primeurs*, your December peas, your January asparagus?'

'We should eat them ourselves,' said Nicole, sternly.

'You might do that now; but I do not think that eating them would pay you for all they cost you,' said Yseulte, not very sure of her ground, and therefore timid in treading it.

'We should not grow them; there would be no need to grow them,' said Nicole, obstinately. 'Everybody would have his cabbage in his pot if there were not those pestilent aristocrats and rich folks.'

'But you might plant cabbages now,' insisted her *pétiote*. 'Why should you not plant cabbages everywhere now if you like? Only you always say it is only the *primeurs* that pay well.'

'Oh, *ma mie*, you belong to them, so you defend them!' grumbled her foster-mother, finding the argument go against her. 'And what are they going to do with you? Cut off all your beautiful hair, and cram you between four stone walls all your life, because it suits their pride to get rid of you!'

'One cannot live better than in God's service,' said Yseulte, with a passing blush.

'Oh, yes, one can,' muttered Nicole, 'when one is sixteen years old and has a face like yours; one could have a gallant lover, and a loyal lord, a home of one's own, and children one after another at one's breast.'

A colour like that of the red winter roses which she was binding up for the Nice markets came into the girl's cheeks.

'I am quite happy to dedicate my life to our Mother and her poor,' she said, in that tone which always awed and silenced Nicole. 'All that I fear is, not to be worthy. There have been holy women of my race. I may never content them as they watch me from their places at God's right hand.'

The coarse blunt fashion of speech of her foster-mother, and the crude class-hatreds and political animosities which Nicole had imbibed from her husband often pained and offended the delicacy and the pride of the girl; but the rough woman loved her, was almost the only creature that did love her, save some of the younger children in the convent; and Yseulte bore with her faults with that indulgent affection which is not blind, but patient and ever forgiving.

She spoke in simplicity and sincerity; she had been so drilled to behold her only future in the religious life, that she prayed night and day to be worthy of such election; and if a thrill of longing for unknown freedom, for unimaginable joys, sometimes came over her she loyally stifled it ere it could grow to any strength. From her babyhood she had been taught to consider herself consecrated to the Church, and that knowledge had always kept her a little apart from others, made her more serious, more sensitive, more meditative, than her age usually is.

'And, to be sure, if there be any up there who do know, it is a crying shame that they do not interfere,' muttered her foster-mother, only half abashed. But Yseulte did not hear her; she had let the roses lie on her lap, her hands were motionless, her eyes were looking far away, farther than the snow which crowned the distant mountains; she was thinking of that saint by whom her childhood had been sheltered; could it indeed be that so great a love as her grandmother's had been had perished utterly, had gone whither it knew nothing, saw nothing, had no power to warn or save? If it were so, she was alone indeed. But——

'Nay, do not think of them,' said Nicole, roughly; 'what is dead is dead, my sweet; be it a pig or be it a princess, when the life is out the sense is out with it; it rots, but it does not wake.'

'Hush!' said the girl, with a little frown and a sense of pain, as if she had heard some foul irreverence. The dead were all she had to care for; half her young life was passed in thinking of them, in praying for them, in wondering if they approved that which she did. 'Christ will give you your dower,' her grandmother had said often to her, a little seven-year-old child, who had vaguely understood that her future was pledged to heaven; and that she must never be fractious, or noisy, or sullen, or give way to appetite or mischief as other children did who were less honoured. It had made her neither affected nor hypocritical; only pathetically doubtful of herself and capable of repressing her naturally buoyant spirits with an incredible patience which was almost heroism, but went always unrewarded.

Faïel was a part of the old world of Bretagne, where the land is green and deeply wooded, and the days are misty and soft and still; it lies inland, and has no sight of the sea; it is traversed by narrow roads sunk down low between moss-grown walls of verdure; it seems all covered up with moss and ferns and boughs; there is always moisture in the air and there are almost always clouds in the sky, but it is a sweet, tender, if mournful country, and in the late-arriving spring becomes a very bower of flowers.

In the heart of this green country the ancient village of Faïel held the equally ancient convent of the Holy Ladies of St. Anne, with its long grey stone walls, its steep shining metal roofs, and its high belfry with its cross of gilded brass towering above the low quaint cottages which crept humbly up beneath it many centuries ago. The foundation owed its origin to Anne of Bretagne herself, and year after year, century after century, undisturbed by wars or revolutions, and unreached by any change of thought or manners the pious ladies of Faïel, in their habits of black and white, had reared the young daughters of the Breton nobility and gentry in the ways of God and in such secular learning as seemed not too profane. The community was severe in its rules and austerely simple in all its customs; but the children were happy if not gay; the green, leafy, silent country was between them and the world, the sisters were kind and gentle, the young girls murmured together, joyously, unreproved, like young swallows chirping under the eaves in midsummer. This holy house in pious Morbihan was wholly unlike those fashionable convents of Paris, and near it, where all the pomps and vanities of the world find their way, and its jealousies and its rivalries fret and fume in miniature mimicry. The Dames de Ste. Anne had all the primitive faiths, the unblemished loyalties, the devout beliefs in tradition of the Middle Ages; they taught the history of France from religious instead of secular records, and the history of the saints from the Golden Legend; they worked silver lilies on white banners, and in their chapel every day a Mass was said for Henri Cinq. Their little maidens became under their hands simple, earnest, grave, and most innocent and truthful creatures, ignorant, no doubt, in many things, but possessing a perfect courage and a beautiful candour; such maidens as in the old days, from the Combât des Trente to Quiberon, had become the wives and mothers of the Breton seigneurie, and had, if need were, defended a castle and headed a sally of men-at-arms in the holy cause of their duke or of their king; women like the arum lilies that covered the damp green earth in their native woods; women whose eyes look at us still, serious and serene, from the gold blazonries of illuminated missals, where their miniatures have been painted beneath their scutcheons and their crowns.

Of these children, when they had passed from the gates of Faïel for the last time, some went to pass all their years in the small secluded châteaux or the dull stone-built towns of the seashore or the interior; some, finding a wider flight, a bolder fate, went into the life of the world and lived that life. But wherever they went, whatever they became, none of them ever wholly forgot Faïel; all of them when they bore children said, as they looked on their little daughters, 'They shall go to the Dames de Ste. Anne;' so that generation after generation came to the great Gothic gateway, and passed within and dwelt there for eight or ten peaceful years; and the sisters, though death made changes amidst them, yet seemed always the same.

Yseulte, who was a fanciful child like most of those who have a lonely childhood, used to believe that they were like that woman of the time of Clovis who learned the secret of eternal life from listening to the singing of the forest birds.

She used to look through the grating down the deep green shade of the woods without, and think, 'That is why they live so long, why they are always content.'

One day an old peasant, who was called a witch in Faïel, saw her looking so and heard her say something of her thoughts to her companion, and the old crone shook her head wisely, 'Do not wish to live long; wish to live so that you have all heaven in one hour; it is not the birds, nor is it the woods, nor is it the saints, that will give you that.'

'What does she mean?' said Yseulte.

'In the village they say she has been a wicked woman,' said the girl who was beside her.

Yseulte pondered often on the mysterious words, but she could never understand them.

At Faïel her days and years went by without any sorrow, if without any pleasure save such as youth and perfect health and willingness to accomplish all allotted tasks can bring with them. She always wore grey or black or white; no colours were ever seen, no ornaments were ever allowed within the sacred walls. She was regarded as certain to enter the religious life. *'Tu seras des nôtres,'* said the nuns so often to her that before she was ten years old she had grown so imbued with the idea that she had never dreamed of resisting such a destination. Her life was so entirely simple, in a way so barren, that the spiritual world assumed a proportion in it which would have been morbid had not the high courage and bodily healthfulness of her resisted the gloom which those who had to do with her deemed most fitting to the loneliness of her lot. She came of a race of gay nobles, of reckless soldiers, of high-handed seigneurs, and some instincts of their courage, of their temper, of their imprudence, stirred in her now and then beneath the calm of cloistral habit and the spirituality of her natural temperament.

'Do you think the daughter of Gui de Valogne will ever be a saint?' the Duc de Vannes often said to his wife. He thought that blood would out even beneath the coif of a Carmelite. His wife replied that the Valogne had always kept their women pure, if at the sword's point, and that amongst them there had been more than one canonised; besides, she added, Yseulte was a child both grave and good; she would never know the world or its temptations; she would live and die as a lily did in a convent garden.

The Duc shrugged his shoulders:

'She has her father's blood in her,' he said, 'and he would have suited no cloister but Roissy or Medmenham.'

He believed in very few things, but his one belief was his conviction that the bias of a race goes with it as do its diseases or its excellences. Most racing men are implicit believers in hereditary influence, and the Duc, who had bred winners at Chantilly and at Ascot, did not credit that the daughter of Gui de Valogne would contentedly become a Ste. Catherine or a Sœur Rose.

'Of course you may shut her perforce in a religious house; so might you shut her in a coffin. To be sure, the one murder is legal and the other would not be so,' he said, with some ill-humour, the night after Othmar noticed his young cousin with her long black gloves, her stately curtsy, her sash à l'enfant, and her beautiful figure, which had the slimness of a child and the promise of a goddess.

'I believe you are almost in love with her yourself,' said the Duchess.

'I wonder no one else is wholly,' he answered, with petulance; and he wrote to his jeweller in the Rue de la Paix for a locket, a girl's locket; something with pearls. He thought even a Mother Superior could hardly object to pearls.

Yseulte, all unconscious of the perilous honour projected for her by her cousin's lord, passed the whole day up at the little church, arranging the flowers which Othmar had given her in the morning, and others which his men, by his orders, had brought thither in the forenoon. She was happier than she had been since her grandmother had died. A warm human interest had come suddenly into the monotony and solitude of her existence. She worked at the decoration of the little place with ardour and delight. She had never before possessed such flowers as these; the woods had yielded all those which had ever decked the altar of the chapel at Faïel. She had only seen such gorgeous blossoms as these in the glass-house at Millo, where she would no more have dreamed of gathering them than of wearing her cousin's diamonds.

'He shall see how beautiful it looks to-morrow,' she thought with each blossom that she added, each leaf she touched. That he would come she never doubted; a promise, ever such a little one, was so sacred to herself that for any pledge to be forgotten would have seemed to her quite impossible.

The old vicar came and went, the sacristan and the housekeeper stood and chattered and told her for the hundredth time all their household troubles;

the gay sunshine streamed in past the open door and through the dulled grey glass of the small windows, a goat trotted up the aisle and nibbled at the bay boughs which she had tied together. The morning passed like a pleasant dream; it seemed not December to her but May. She was but a child, and for once the weight of her future fell off her young shoulders. She laughed,—softly, because she sat on the altar steps,—but she laughed. 'God is so good,' she thought, in the simple sincerity of her glad gratitude.

'You will let me sing, my reverend, at all the offices?' she said to the old man when she had finished her welcome labours and stood with him within the stone porch whilst the sun was setting.

'Surely, my child,' he said willingly. 'It does me good to hear your voice, and I think it must even be pleasant to the angels too.'

She went happily along the uneven little path which led down the hill under great olive trees and warm evening sunset skies to Millo. Her feet went so rapidly that the maid whose duty it was to attend her out of doors could ill keep pace with her. Her heart was so light; she had the vision of the beautiful flowers always before her eyes, of the altar which she had made like a garden. It mattered nothing to her that when she entered the house she was met by a reprimand, that she found her simple supper cold, that her little cousins were malicious, quarrelsome, unkind; all those were trifles. She bore them with perfect patience, and with never a word of harsh reply; and she went to her bed and slept soundly, dreaming of roses and lilies, and S. Cecilia, and of a world of angels who leaned on the sunbeams as on golden spears, and looked down on her and smiled.

She was up long before the first gleam of coming day lightened the eastward seas. No one ever forbade her going to the church as often as she chose; they deemed it in unison with her future vocation. She had attached herself to this rude, lonely, little place in the winters which she had passed there under the charge of Nicole Sandroz. Her cousin had said once that it would be better if she attended instead the offices of the house chapel, but she had not insisted, and the child, who had a certain obstinacy in her affections, had persevered in her loyalty to the parish church under its silvery mist of olives.

This morning her foster-mother was in waiting to accompany her. The cold was keen in the greyness of the dawn; the sun, which at noon would vivify the winter landscape to summer-like warmth, was still hidden in the nether world, the earth and the sea were dark, the stars still lingered in the shadowy skies.

'What folly, *pétiote*!' muttered Nicole, who had her lanthorn, 'to get up out of your bed to go and sing an ave! If it were to pack a crate of oranges there would be some sense!'

'Hush, please,' said Yseulte gently. 'Perhaps grandmère hears.'

The memory of the old Marquise always touched and silenced the irreligious grumbling of Nicole. She said nothing more, but toiled on stoutly, her lanthorn twinkling amongst the rough grass, white with passing frost.

'The child would be best in her bed,' she thought; 'but there is one thing,—she never takes cold. One would like to think the saints had a care of her, but that is all rubbish; even our mayor says so now, and he is such a dunderhead, what he cannot stomach nobody can.'

Still Nicole, who came to Mass for her sake, though the good woman in her soul hated the bigots, the black beetles, of the church, held on her way up the hill, stumbling over the roots of the old olives; it pleased the *pétiote* that she should come, and after all it could do no harm.

Eager, proud, joyous—more joyous she feared than was meet for the sanctity of the hour and the errand—Yseulte led her into the church as the first pale light of daybreak spread itself over the earth.

'Now you will see how beautiful it is!' she murmured to Nicole.

Alas, the fair garden she had made and left at twilight was a ruin now! Where she had caused the metal and the wood and the stone to bloom as with the blossoms of Paradise, there were only poor pale yellow withered things colourless as ashes!

The frost of the night had stolen the glory from the flowers as the hand of the Church would strike the youth from her life and leave it hard and dumb as a stone. The blossoms had died of cold like little children lost in the snow, like bright butterflies beaten down and drowned in a storm of hail.

A low pathetic cry of grief escaped her as she saw the lovely things, which she so ignorantly and innocently had slain, hanging their folded petals in the chill glimmer of the early day as the limbs of infants hang in death.

Her eyes filled with hot quick tears that ran down her cheeks.

'Oh, look! Oh, look!' she cried piteously.

'What could you expect, *pétiote*,' said Nicole with rough sympathy, 'if you bring hothouse flowers from under their glass? Our nights are cold—my man said last night it was two below zero by the mercury tube in our wall. Do not cry, *mignonne*; you could not help it; you did not think of it; children never do think. But bay and laurel and all those common shrubs are best fit to stand the cold of the church. These things are only aristocrats.'

Nicole checked herself; she remembered the Marquise de Creusac, with the frost of poverty and cruel loss upon her, meeting misfortune with serene courage and unchanging dignity; her comparison, she saw, halted and failed.

Yseulte did not hear; she was thinking piteously, 'And I did so want him to see how beautiful it all looked through his kindness!'

She was quite sure that Othmar would come to one office or another during the day. She was ashamed to be so occupied with this one thought when the drone of the acolyte was chanting in monotonous sing-song the opening words of the Mass; but it was stronger than herself. She thought of nothing else, to her own surprise and confusion; she was wholly unable to keep her mind to the holy offices of the hour; for the first time, the sonorous Latin words failed to carry her soul with them; she was glancing while she knelt at the closed rickety door, she was wondering whilst she sang the 'Agnus Dei,' would he come? She had taken such infinite pains with the flowers, and now all their beauty was gone!—they were only faded, helpless-looking melancholy wrecks of themselves, disfiguring the altar rather than lending it grace and glory.

'*Pauvre pétiote!*' thought Nicole, fingering her beads, and bending her stiff knees from habit. 'The frost will come just like that to her, and nobody will care. Often have I a mind to go up to Millo and tell them it is a shame, a vile shame; but they would not care, they would have me turned out for an old mad woman.'

The church was very dark; the few lights there were did not dissipate the shadows of the dawn; the clear melodious voice of Yseulte rose in the gloom as a nightingale's does in the lovelier dusk of a midsummer daybreak.

All her heart thrilled out in it, and when the last notes sank to silence there was a tremor as of tears in them.

Nicole's heart swelled too as she heard, half with pain, half with rage.

'I would sooner she were singing "do', do', l'enfant dor'!" by her baby's cradle,' thought this heathen.

She attended every office of the church during the next twelve hours, but Othmar came not to one of them. With Vespers all hope of seeing him there—such a vague, innocent, half-conscious hope as it was—had perished quite, like the orchids on the altar.

The day was over: the church had once more no light except that of its twinkling candles; the peasants shuffled to their feet and clattered out over the stones; Nicole began to chatter to the maid; the old vicar had tottered into the sacristy and was pulling off his vestments; the last office was done; the butterfly orchids were dying in the stench of the sputtering candlewicks; the acolyte—a ploughboy in a short linen tunic which showed his hobnailed boots—began to put the wicks out with a brass extinguisher fixed at the end of a long stick; she thought she would never bring flowers there any more—it was cruel—they withered and faded, and who could tell what they might suffer? She had never remembered that before.

The flowers had died in the service of the church; so would she. It had seldom seemed hard before.

While the two women chattered in low tones of the doings of Millo, she turned quickly back to the altar-steps and knelt down there and said one last prayer confusedly, conscious that she had been at fault all through the Mass in thinking of other things than the holy services in which she had taken part.

She rose, with the tears in her eyes, and went out through the little dark aisle between the two women, leaving the poor lost flowers in a confused and shadowy mass upon the altar until dawn, to be tossed away and thrust out under the sacristan's broom to the dust-heap. Othmar had not come.

He was sitting at his own table, with the Princess Napraxine at his right hand.

The girl could see the lighted windows of his château as she walked down under the olives through the dusky furrows, already dotted with blades of corn, the women still chattering as they came behind her, the woods of Millo black under the moon, the stars shining, a distant watchdog giving tongue.

'You are late, *pétiote*,' said her foster-mother, kissing her hand at the door of the house. 'But it will not matter; they are all dining at Count Othmar's; if no one of those cats of gouvernantes tell the Duchesse, she will be none the wiser.'

'There is nothing to conceal,' cried Yseulte a little coldly. 'My cousin knows that I go out to Vespers as well as Mass. Good night.'

She kissed her nurse on the cheek, and went up the staircase of Millo. Her heart had contracted with a sort of pang as she heard the idle words, 'They are all dining at Count Othmar's.' She did not wonder that he had not invited her; no one invited her anywhere; she was a schoolgirl now, and would be a nun later on; she had nothing to do with the world, and yet her heart ached a little.

She did not touch the coffee and the cakes that her maid brought her. She sat at the window of her own little room, and looked every now and then out into the chilly night and across the moonlit landscape to the towers of S. Pharamond. There were points of light of all colours sparkling in the darkness round the château. They were the lamps of his gardens, which were illuminated down to the very edge of the sea. She felt a great longing to cry like a little child; but she would not yield to it. Only two great tears rolled slowly down her cheeks. She knew that she had been very foolish to expect him at the church; only he had said that he would come!——

# CHAPTER XI.

A few mornings later, after his noonday breakfast, Alain de Vannes sauntered out into the rose gardens of his wife, having seen there the figure of his wife's young cousin in her demure grey dress with the cape of sable, which he was just then in the mood to think the prettiest female garb in the world. He went up to her with easy and good-humoured courtesy, as became her kinsman and her host.

'My cousin,' he said tenderly, 'you have no trinkets and pretty things, as a little lady of your years should have. I believe there are all that are left of the Valogne jewels waiting for you in strong coffers, but meantime here is a little bird that will whisper to you pretty things if you will listen to him. You may wear a dove, you know, at the convent itself. It is the bird of the Holy Spirit.'

And with that he gave her what he had telegraphed for from Paris, a locket of blue enamel rimmed with pearls, and a dove, made of pearls, flying on it; it hung from a thick gold chain.

She was so astonished that she could not speak.

The Duc watched her with amusement. 'Pardieu!' he thought, 'it is much more entertaining to give to the *ingénue* than to the *belle petite*. What wonder, what delight, what innocent gratitude!—and the others only box your ears if the diamonds be not big enough or the emeralds do not please them. Really we are fools.'

Yseulte meanwhile had not spoken yet; what moved her so intensely was not the gift of the medallion itself, splendid though it was, but the idea that anyone had had so much remembrance of her. She had scarcely had more notice than a careless bow or a brief *'bon jour'* from her cousin's husband in all her life, and now, he brought her this magnificent present! And yet, how much sooner she would have had Othmar remember to go and hear her sing!

'Well, *mignonne*,' said the Duc gaily. 'You look as if you were not sure whether you were in earth or in heaven. *We* are not, when we look at you.'

'It is most good of you; it is most beautiful,' she said, with hesitation. 'That you should have thought of me is so kind; but I fear I ought not to wear it; you know in two years' time I am to enter the Carmelite communion.'

'Nonsense! It is the bird of the Holy Spirit,' said de Vannes, with an ambiguous smile. 'I think you may wear it when you are an abbess—if ever you be an abbess. Ah, my child, it is a cruel thing to doom you to the religious life; only ugly women should go there, and you are so handsome, *fillette*,—you will be so handsome!'

'Oh, no!' she said, quickly; she blushed very much; she had been always told that it was a sin to think of any physical charms, and yet she had enough of the instincts of a beautiful woman in her to take an unconscious delight in the whiteness of her limbs, the thickness of her hair, the smile of her own eyes from a mirror.

'Oh, yes!' said de Vannes, still with that smile which vaguely hurt her. 'You will be marvellously handsome, Yseulte; I think that is the chief reason why the ladies wish you in the cloister! It was certainly the reason why they would not take you to Othmar's last night. To be sure you are not in the world, but in the country they might have made an exception; you are seen in our drawing-rooms.'

She lifted her eyes with eager appeal. 'Did he ask me? Did he think of me?' she said, under her breath.

The keen glance of the Duc flashed over her face, and grew harsh and suspicious.

'Because he spoke to you once,' he thought, 'I suppose, though you be a young saint in embryo, you are not proof against his millions! You are all alike after all, you women, even in the bud.'

Aloud he said: 'Yes; I believe Othmar bade my wife bring you. Perhaps she thought it was too much like the great world for you; it was a brilliant affair—all done for the Princess Napraxine.'

'Who is the Princess Napraxine?' she asked, surprised at her own temerity.

'She is the lady of Othmar's dreams,' said de Vannes, with an unkind satisfaction. 'You are sure to see her here sometime. What did you think of him the other night? You know, I suppose, that he could buy up all France if he chose.'

'I did not know,' she murmured. 'Nicole, I think, said that he was rich.'

'Rich!' echoed the Duc, with derision. 'That is not a word to describe Othmar. He has about a million millions, and he would probably be happier if he were the blind beggar of the Pont Neuf. His millions do not do anything for him with Nadine Napraxine, and it is only for Nadine Napraxine that he exists.'

Then he paused; the respect for *la jeune fille*, by which the most dissolute of his countrymen is restrained from long habit, making him repress the sentence he had on his lips; that momentary flush and light of happiness at being remembered by Othmar which he had seen on his young cousin's face had made him bitter against his neighbour and friend, and he would willingly have continued his sarcasms on a man who, with all the world at his feet, cared only for another man's wife, who laughed at him.

Yseulte listened with serious and wistful eyes; she did not know enough of his meaning, nor enough of the sympathy which had attracted her towards Othmar, to understand why she felt a vague pain at hearing these things said of him mingled with a delighted gratitude that he had remembered her. It was not to have gone to his party that she cared for, but to be remembered by him.

The children and their governesses approached her at that moment, and the Duc somewhat hurriedly turned away.

'Do not let these fools see your locket,' he said quickly, meaning by that epithet the wise women who educated his daughters. 'If Cri-Cri notice it, tell her, of course.'

Yseulte, surprised at the injunction, looked at him in wonder; but she saw so much irritation in his expression that, being accustomed to obey the orders of others without comment, and to be taught that silence was one of the first of duties, she put his gift in her pocket as the children approached, and their father, with a petulant word or two, turned away, lighting a cigar.

'What was *petit papa* saying to you?' cried the little sisters in a breath.

They were pretty children, with clouds of hair and saucy peevish little faces. They wore sailor dresses, made very short at the knee and showing legs very shapely though too thin. Blanchette was blonde; Toinon was a little darker and rosier. Blanchette was the more elegant and the more witty by far; Toinon was the sturdier and the naughtier. But Toinon had still something of childhood left in her; Blanchette had lost every atom of hers years before, though she was only ten years old now. Toinon loved horses, dogs, boats, and *le sport* generally; Blanchette only cared for smart frocks, things which cost a great deal of money, scandal which she overheard, and which fascinated her in proportion as it was unintelligible to her, and the sense that she was looked at admiringly as she drove behind the ponies in the Bois or walked, with a court of small boys behind her, down the planks at Trouville.

Between her two cousins and Yseulte de Valogne there was a great gulf fixed, that gulf into which there has fallen so much of the innocence of youth, of the grace of good manners, of the charm of girlhood, and of the obligation of nobility; that gulf over which modern society dances so lightly, blind and indifferent to all it has lost.

'What was *petit papa* saying?' cried Blanchette and Toinon in one breath, their eyes wide open with curiosity and sparkling with suspicion.

Yseulte hesitated; she scarcely knew what to say, and a kind of oppression came upon her with the sense of the gift and the secret which she had to keep and conceal.

'He was telling me that I was invited—there—last night,' she said, as she looked across at the trees of S. Pharamond; 'but they thought me not old enough,' she added, with an unconscious sigh.

Blanchette turned up her little delicate nose in the air.

'*Grande nigaude, va!*' she said contemptuously. 'You will never be anything but a big baby, you! When I am as old as you, I shall have been married a whole year to a crown prince, and have gone to all the theatres, and read all the newspapers—every one!'

'But she will never see a newspaper, and never go to a theatre; never, never, never,—a big never!' cried Toinon, who was two years younger than Blanchette, as she clapped her hands and capered.

'She does not care, she is such a stupid,' said Blanchette, with all the superiority of measureless scorn.

'Papa was giving you something: what did he give you?' said Toinon. 'He said you were handsome the other night to mamma, I heard him. Mamma was angry.'

'Mamma did not care,' said Blanchette. 'If it had been the Marquis Raymond!'——

Then the little sisters laughed.

Yseulte with difficulty escaped from her little tormentors, and wandered alone through the pretty grounds; while the closed shutters of the villa of Millo showed that her cousin and her house-party were still sleeping after the cotillon with which Othmar's party had closed; an improvised and unexpected cotillon, for which, nevertheless, there had been all manner of admirable surprises, marvellous novelties, and costly presents.

When she was quite alone she took out her pearl medallion and looked at it with all a child's rapture at a toy and something of a woman's pleasure in a jewel. The kindness of her cousin de Vannes overwhelmed her. She had known him now and then, as she passed the doors of the billiard-room, or watched the drag roll out of the courtyard, give her a careless, good-tempered nod and a lazy word or two, but never any more notice than that, which was as much as Blanchette and Toinon ever received from him. At such times as he had come down to Bois le Roy or Millo, when she was there, she had heard of him as a man only devoted to horses and dogs, to sport of all sorts, to his stag-hounds and boar-hounds and otter-hounds, to his coach and his stud and his great *chasses*; she knew that he was a very grand gentleman in Paris, and at Bois le Roy—despite all revolutions—was a kind of king. And he had thought about her so much that he had bought her a locket! She could scarcely believe it.

She sat in a little nook made by magnolias that overhung the sea, and saw the sun shine on her dove of pearls, and wondered if she would dare to wear it; would the Duchess approve of it? There was only one thing which disturbed her, it was his recommendation to silence; there had been a look in his eyes, too, when he had said, 'You are very handsome, *fillette*,' which haunted her with a vague uneasiness. She was too utterly innocent to be alarmed by it, but a certain instinct in her shrank from the remembrance of that regard. It was the first look of sensual admiration which had been ever given her, and though he had added 'Of course you must tell Cri-Cri,' he had said it grudgingly, as though he would willingly, if he could have ventured to do so, have bidden her keep his gift a secret from his wife.

'Are you counting your jewels, Mademoiselle de Valogne?' said the voice of Othmar. 'Leave that until you are thirty years older and need their aid.'

Without any thought of her he had been strolling on the rocks above the little harbour which belonged equally to S. Pharamond and to Millo. He had been bathing and swimming, and was returning to his house, when he caught sight of her seated beneath the magnolias.

Yseulte coloured, and rose to her feet, dropping the medallion in her surprise as his voice startled her from her meditation. Othmar picked it up and returned it to her.

'What a happy trinket to hold your thoughts so long,' he said as he did so. 'I have been watching you for a quarter of an hour, and you have never ceased to look at that most fortunate jewel.'

'My cousin, the Duc de Vannes, gave it to me a moment ago,' she answered him, vexed that he should suppose she could care so much for any trifle.

'De Vannes!' echoed Othmar in some surprise; 'I did not know he had so much good taste in the selection either of his gifts or their recipients. It is a very pretty medallion,' he added, noticing her look of distress and of bewilderment. 'The dove is admirably done; I hope it will be an emblem of the peace which will always remain with you.'

She did not speak; the quick sensitiveness of her instincts made her feel the satire of his felicitations, and become conscious that for some reason or another he disapproved the gift which she had received.

'I have never had any present before from anyone,' she said simply, 'so it is a great pleasure to me. I do not mean only because it is pretty——'

'But because of the affection it represents? I understand,' said Othmar, while he thought to himself, 'That *goailleur* de Vannes!—must he even bring his indecencies to Millo and try and corrupt a poor helpless child? The man would not spend twenty francs out of mere good nature, nor look at her twice out of mere compassion.'

He looked at her himself now where she sat under the magnolia branches; and it seemed to him as if she were the dove and he saw the hawk descending. Alain de Vannes could be seductive when he chose; he was good-looking and extremely distinguished, was accustomed to conquest, and had that charm of manner which the habit of the world and the society of women make second nature. If his fancy had lighted on his wife's cousin he would not be likely to pause because she was penniless, lonely, and consecrated to a spiritual life.

'One ought to put her on her guard, and yet, who could venture to do that,' he thought; he, at all events, had no title to do so, and if he had, he could not willingly have been the first to tell her that under the roses there were vipers, that behind the dew and the sunrise there were evil fires burning.

'Will you stay long at Millo?' he asked abruptly.

'I came here for two months,' she said. 'We were all sent away,—there was fever; I have been here often before. I am very fond of Millo.'

'Why would they not let you honour me last night?'

'I do not go into the world at all. I never shall.' She hesitated a moment, then added timidly, 'It was very kind to think of me.'

'It would not be easy to forget you,' said Othmar with a sincerity which surprised himself. 'I wish you had been with us; yours is the age for *sauteries* and enjoyment. I should like to see you at your first ball.'

'I shall never go to a ball. It would not be thought right.'

'And do you never rebel against so harsh a destiny?'

She coloured to her eyes as she answered almost inaudibly, 'Sometimes— yes—but then I know that it is I who am wrong and they who are right.'

'Who are they?'

'The Mother Superior; my uncle, de Creusac, by his will; my cousin Aurore; everyone that I belong to at all: my grandmother especially desired it.'

'It makes one wish all the world were agnostic!'

'What did you say?'

Agnostic was not a word she had been allowed to hear.

'I say that it is a cruel thing to force on you such a choice. At least you should be allowed to know what you do, ere you do it. You should see what the world is like before you renounce it. I can fancy that women tired, sorrow-laden, unlovely, unloved, feeble of health, may be glad of the refuge of religious life; but you!——'

'Do you think one should only give God what is weary and worn out?' she said softly. 'Surely one should give one's best?'

Othmar was touched by the words and the tone. To him, whose boyhood had been filled with spiritual faiths and hopes, and whose manhood had the pain of knowledge that all these gracious myths and wistful desires were but mere dreams, there was the echo of remembered adorations, of exquisite unreasoning beliefs, in the simple answer which bespoke that faith in heaven which a child has in its mother, unquestioning, undoubting, implicit in obedience and in trust.

Beside the cultured mind of the woman he loved, with its fine scepticism, its delicate ironies, its contemptuous rejections, its intellectual scorn, no doubt this simple, narrow, unintelligent faith was foolish and childish, and out of date; yet it touched him; in Yseulte de Valogne it had an unconscious heroism, a beautiful repose, which lifted it out of the cramped rigidity of creeds and the apathy of ignorance.

There were beneath her gravity and spirituality a warmth, a vitality, a latent force, which seemed to him to cry aloud for enjoyment and expansion. Sooner or later all that teeming life slumbering in her would awake and demand its common rights; no creature perfectly organised and full of health and strength can forego the natural joys of human existence without suffering a thousand deaths. As yet, no doubt, she was as innocent, as ignorant, of the tyranny of the senses, as any shell that lay at the bottom of the blue waters yonder. She might have fallen from heaven that day for aught she knew of all which, in her unconsciousness, she was ready to renounce. But any hour that divine innocence might be destroyed by a word, banished at a touch. Alain de Vannes, or any other, might choose to find sport in waking and in slaying it; and then, how unhappy she would be! How like a bird freshly captured, and beating itself to death against the bars!

It was only in France that a high-born and beautiful girl could be sacrificed thus because she had no dower. Everywhere else women without dowers were sought and taken in marriage every day. As if a few hundred thousand francs were needful to make youth, and loveliness, and purity, and high lineage, acceptable to men!

'You know my cousin the Duc very well?' she said timidly after a long silence.

'We have lived in the same world; I have not been intimate with him.'

'Do you think he would be very vexed if I asked Nicole—that is, my foster-mother—to sell this locket for me?'

'I fear he would not be best pleased. Why should you wish to sell it?'

She hesitated, then answered: 'I want to buy the vicar that new gown he wants so much. He will never spend a centime on himself, and his gown has been mended and mended and mended; it is all a patchwork, and even that is dropping to pieces, and the bishop's visitation is near at hand. I thought the value of this locket would buy a priest's gown, if my cousin de Vannes would not be angry.'

'That is a pretty thought of you; it would certainly buy many *soutanes*,' said Othmar. 'But I think Alain would not be at all pleased if you sold his present; and I told you the other day that I will give the curé a new gown myself with the very utmost pleasure. You say that I belong to his parish.'

She smiled; nevertheless, she hesitated to accept his offer.

'You must have so many things to give. Nicole says that people are always asking you for things.'

'They do not always get them,' replied Othmar, with a smile. 'If they wished only for such useful and harmless things as *soutanes*, they should always have their wish.'

'Are you so immensely rich then?' she asked him, opening widely her golden-brown eyes, which looked as if the sunshine was always shining in them.

'To my misfortune,' said Othmar, annoyed. Could not even a child of sixteen out of a convent forget his riches? Was it possible she too was going to ask him for something?

She looked at him gravely.

'I wonder you do not build a cathedral,' she said, after a pause.

'A cathedral!' he echoed, in surprise. 'I would if I had the faith of those who used to do so.'

'It is what I would do if I had money,' said she, still very gravely. 'I would build one in the heart of a forest, with the deer and the birds all round it; not jammed up amongst streets and crowds like Nôtre Dame or Chartres.'

Then a sudden sense came over her that she was violating all the rules of propriety by which her life was ordered in thus speaking out her thoughts to one who was almost a stranger; in tarrying at all by the side of a man who was of no parentage to her. She rose, a little hurriedly, but with the stately grace which was natural to her; the grace of old Versailles and Marly.

'I think I must go back to the house,' she said, with a little shyness. 'My cousin does not like me to be alone, or to talk to anyone——'

'The Duchesse will not object to me,' said Othmar, with the same smile as he had had when using the same words a few days before. 'Besides, Mademoiselle, you are in another world than your convent. At Millo men are not thought dragons and tigers. We are poor creatures, indeed, but harmless; more injured than injuring. Do not be so alarmed. I want you to tell me a great deal more about our vicar. Where am I to get his measure for his gown? Will he be surprised with it? Will you not let me send it to you that you may take it to him? I should be ashamed to do so. I have never been inside his church, even to hear you sing.'

'No, you never came yesterday!' she said, with a sigh, innocently revealing that she had remarked his absence with regret.

'To my shame and loss, I did not. I had my uncle with me all the day, and at night a dinner, a concert, and the *sauterie*, to which I hoped you would have been brought.'

'But I cannot dance,' said the child, blushing very much as she made the humiliating confession.

'So much the better,' said Othmar, inconsistently, 'I am sure, however, that you would dance with admirable grace if you danced at all. Anyone who moves well can dance well.'

This time the colour in her cheeks was that of pleasure at his praise. She was silent, looking at him a little wistfully, recalling what De Vannes had said of the Princess Napraxine.

The kindliness of his tone, its mingling of familiarity and reverence, melted her reserve and disarmed her shyness. There had been that in the compliment of Alain de Vannes which had startled and alarmed her; but in the almost paternal gentleness and friendliness of Othmar's words there was nothing to do so. He had little to her of the chillness and languid irony which often frightened even women in him, whilst he had all the graceful courtesy of a man polished by all the habits of the great world, and accustomed to that pre-eminence which gives supreme ease of manner. To her Othmar seemed a hero, a king, an ideal among men; when her cousin had said to her that this person, so powerful, so great, and so rich, was also unhappy, he had said the only thing needed to complete his fascination for her and to make him the master of her dreams.

He bowed low before her with a sense of something holier than was often met with in this world, and looked after her as she sped over the lawns to the house.

'A beautiful creature, with a tender heart in her breast,' he thought. 'Why could I not meet her and find my heaven in possessing her, instead of caring only for a woman who has no more passion or pity than those Mexican aloes?'

As he walked home the remembrance of Nadine Napraxine seemed like a little adder growing in his heart, and the large eyes of Yseulte de Valogne seemed to look into his soul with their golden sun-rays. He was passionately in love with the one, bitterly, angrily, resentfully, in love; for the other he felt an extreme pity, a sympathy, which with propitious circumstances might become affection, an admiration of the senses which might with time be heightened to desire, an inclination to take her in his arms and save her from her fate as he might have taken up a wounded bird to save it from the trap.

———————

# CHAPTER XII.

Yseulte the next day was sitting writing a German theme in the children's room, of which the windows opened on the gardens, when Alain de Vannes, with a cigarette in his mouth, pushed open the glass door and sauntered in from the open air.

'Well, my cousin,' he said gaily. 'Here you are, shut up like a little mouse. What nonsense it is! German? What good will that do you? When the *revanche* comes, we shall speak with bullets and they will understand as we understood. Pardieu! When they burnt my woods in Charente!—I had a ball in my ribs at Saarbrück; did you know it? Where were you? In Paris?—during the siege? A baby like you! Is it possible!'

'There were many other little children there,' said the girl with a shudder; she had been such a little child then, that the horror of the time had left an ineffaceable mark upon her.

'Of course, of course,' said the Duc, seating himself on the edge of the table. 'But not many of your rank. Most people got away. Ah, to be sure, I remember your uncles de Creusac were both shot; yes, we all lost heavily; it is no use thinking of it; but I would give my life to enter Berlin. *Tiens!* this is not what I came to say, but you make one serious; why will you not laugh? Do you know that we have a ball next week?'

'I heard Blanchette saying so.'

'Ah, the little cat! She knows everything. Now, this ball—would you not like to come to it, instead of being shut up in your room writing crabbed German characters?'

'It is impossible.'

While she said the cruel word firmly, her heart gave a great leap of longing that was almost hope.

'Not impossible; perhaps difficult,' said de Vannes, with a smile as he threw his cigar out on to the grass. 'But I think I could persuade Cri-Cri; it is a shame for you to be shut up; you will have enough of that all your life if you go where they say.'

Yseulte was silent; her heart was still beating tumultuously, she breathed quickly.

'How handsome she is!' thought the Duc. 'She only wants that flush of life to be perfect. Women are like alabaster lamps, unlit until they learn envy and desire. When that flame is lighted, then the alabaster glows.'

He stooped his head and kissed her hand, but he did it with a different touch to Othmar's, and she coloured with a sense of pain and anger.

'*Ma mie!*' he murmured. 'I will undertake to combat successfully the scruples of your cousin; you shall see the ball next week. Cri-Cri shall find you a frock, and jewels you want none; you have the supreme jewel—youth; crowns are dull without it; and, let our dear women use what arts they may, they cannot counterfeit it. I will be your good genius, Yseulte, and open your prison doors. You will not refuse me a little gratitude—a little goodwill? Something quite simple and commonplace will content me, you see, but you must give it *de bon cœur.*'

The words were harmless, and said little, but his eyes as they were bent upon her said much; much more than he knew. There was a look in them which lighted their pale blue with a fire from which she shrank by instinct, as from something which scorched and hurt her. The eyes of Alain de Vannes, like those of most men who have lived his life and had his experiences, were cold, jaded, passionless in repose, but when amorous, were cruel, eager, rapacious. Yseulte drew her hand from him; her heart sank five fathoms deep, but she gathered up all her courage.

'You are very good, M. *mon cousin*,' she said with a ceremonious coldness worthy of one twice her years. 'But do not trouble yourself for me. That sort of pleasure would not accord with the life that I am always to lead. I do not know the world; I do not wish to know it; it is never to have anything to do with me; it is better I should not even see it, I might only regret.'

She said the little speech bravely, not faltering once, though to make it cost her a pang, but she crushed out all her natural longings, all her wistful instincts, all her youthful dreams to do so; flowers plucked up by the roots and thrown down at the foot of the altars of Marie. But even at this moment the altar still seemed to her that which she had been always told that it was, a refuge sweet, safe, unfailing. A refuge from what? She did not know, but a vague fear had assailed her.

De Vannes looked at her with surprise and irritation; at the bottom of his heart he was himself ashamed of the unholy wishes which had awakened in him, of the treacherous temptations which he had begun to put in the path of a girl who was his own guest, his wife's relative, and whose position ought in its sheer defencelessness to have been her best safeguard with any man of honour. He was not without honour, in a loose fashion, but he was very unscrupulous when his fancy was excited. If before her retirement to the religious life she should have an 'affaire,' and if that 'affaire' should have himself for its hero, it did not seem to him that anything terrible would have taken place. What was the use of occupying a high position if one could not successfully conduct and cover a little intrigue like that?

At the same time he knew that his designs would scarcely be condoned, even by the very light-minded set amongst which he lived, if it were seriously known that he endeavoured to be the first to corrupt his young cousin. Therefore her words struck a certain nerve of susceptibility within him; he felt a kind of compunction before that serious and guileless regard. Yet he was very angry. He, Alain de Vannes, who never looked at a *fillette*, who never deigned to notice any lesser thing than some of the famous beauties of the great world, or of the half-world, had taken the infinite trouble to distinguish this child, to seek her and to offer her his influence and protection, and she had repulsed him, with her hands lying crossed on her German books and her rose-leaf cheeks growing neither the warmer nor the colder for his regard.

He rose, and his eyebrows contracted in a heavy frown. He was a good-humoured man usually, but in such rare times as his will was crossed he had the petulance and the malice of a spoiled child.

'You are not wise, *fillette*,' he said, with a little laugh. 'I would be a good friend to you, and you may want one before you are safe in the bosom of Our Lady. I wonder the ball did not tempt you. You would have seen your friend Othmar—and Madame Napraxine.'

Then he pulled the glass door open with an impatient hand, and went out into the grounds without, leaving behind him the odour of his cigarette and the sting of his last words.

Blanchette peeped in from behind a silk curtain; her saucy babyish eyes were full of curiosity and wonder.

'*Tiens*, Yseulte,' she said, running up to her cousin, 'I heard all papa said. Why should he want you at the ball, and why should you not go? You are a goose, such a goose! You know papa can always make mamma do what he chooses. He always threatens to send away M. de Prangins.'

Then Blanchette laughed, curling herself up in a little ball at her cousin's feet.

'You should not say such wicked things, Blanchette,' said Yseulte; 'and it is very shameful and dishonourable to listen anywhere unseen——'

Blanchette made a *pied de nez* with her little rosy fingers, with all the mockery and insolence of Gavrôche himself.

'You are vulgar as well as wicked,' said her cousin sadly, as she looked away.

'It is distinguished to be vulgar, now,' said the little ten-year-old Parisienne. 'All the great ladies are, except Madame Napraxine; she is always wrapped up in herself. She has no *entrain*, she cares for nothing. She is not at all my model. Listen! If you were not such an idiot, you would see that *petit papa* is in love with you, ever so much in love! Why don't you get all kinds of things out of him while he is in the humour? He would buy you all the Palais Royal if you knew how to manage him, and mamma will not say anything as long as the Marquis Raymond is here.'

'Blanchette!' cried the girl, indignantly. She rose to her feet; a flood of shame seemed to roll over her.

The insolent, malicious turquoise eyes of Blanchette amused themselves with her horror and trouble.

'You are such a baby!' said the child again, contemptuously. 'You never seem to understand anything. Me, I understand it all. I shall *do* it all when I am married. I shall be just like mamma. It is the Marquis Raymond now; it was the Prince Jacques last year. I liked the Prince Jacques best. He gave me an orchestra of monkeys; you wound it up and all the monkeys played— fife, drum, clarionet, flute, too-too, too-too, tra-la-la-la! The marquis has never given me anything, except a sack of bonbons he might have bought at St. Cloud. If he do not give me something very good at new year, I shall say out loud in the salon, when a lot of people are making visits: "You are not as nice as Prince Jacques!" And how he will look, because he always frets and fumes about the prince! I think they fought about mamma. Oh, it must be such fun to be a woman! I wish, I wish, I wish I were fifteen. I would be so naughty, they would have to marry me to-morrow! If you were not a goose you would be as naughty as ever you could be. They would get you a husband then; papa would see to it.'

'Blanchette!' cried Yseulte, again, in desperation, not knowing how to stem the tide of the child's words. She, like Blanchette herself, was ignorant of all the horrible import of those words which the little thing used, half in malicious precocious knowledge, and half in absolute childish ignorance; but they terrified her and appalled her both in themselves and for their speaker, and for all which, even to her innocence, they suggested of unspeakable inconceivable shamefulness.

'Blanchette!' echoed the child, mimicking the horror and expostulation of her cry. 'Oh, how glad I am I have Schemmitz and Brawn to teach me instead of going to a convent to be made a goose of like you. Schemmitz and Brawn are old owls, but I keep my eyes and my ears open at Trouville, at Biarritz, in Paris, here, anywhere, everywhere. Now, in your nunnery you see no more, you hear no more, than if you were a statue in a chapel. That is why you are so stupid. *Tiens!* Why did papa call Count Othmar your friend? Is he your friend? You are as still as a mouse about everything.'

Her quick glance saw the colour mount into her cousin's face, and the cruel child laughed triumphantly. 'Oh, how you blush, oh-oh! Nobody blushes now-a-days. One must be old-fashioned like you to be so silly. *I* shall never blush. *Tiens*, Yseulte, tell me all about it and I will not tell Toinon.'

'There is nothing to tell,' said Yseulte, almost losing her patience.

'Papa never says anything without meaning something by it,' said Blanchette, sagaciously. 'And if there be nothing, why should you blush? I know all about Count Othmar; he is rich—oh, so rich! Nobody was ever so rich outside the *Juiverie*; I heard them say so this autumn at Aix. But all he cares about is Princess Napraxine. Have you ever seen Princess Napraxine? She drives in the Bois with three horses in the Russian way; the one in the middle is a little in front of the others, and they have only little bits of silver for harness, and they fly—ouf! I mean to marry a Russian.'

'Is she so very beautiful?' said Yseulte, in a low tone, ashamed of questioning the child, and yet impelled by an irresistible desire to hear more of this wondrous sovereign.

'*Pas tant que ça!*' said Blanchette, critically. 'But she is much more than only handsome. She makes every one that goes near her mad about her. She is pale, and has great eyes; but there is no one like her, they say. What do you think they call her? They call her Flocon de Neige. She cares for nobody, you know; that is what they mean. She is not at all what I admire; what I admire is the Duchesse d'Ambrée. *Elle sait se faire une tête!*—continued Blanchette, growing breathless, and powerless to express her immense admiration.

Madame d'Ambrée was a blonde, with a profusion of real gold curls, cheeks admirably tinted, and a tiny Cupid's bow of a mouth; a great huntress, a great swimmer, a great smoker; she had very extravagant toilettes, and very loud manners, and was a really great lady, with the language of a cantinière: she was the object of the child's idolatry.

'I will be just like that,' Blanchette said to herself whenever she saw Madame d'Ambrée walking on the planks at Trouville, going into the casino at Aix, or driving her piebald ponies round the Bois. Blanchette admired her own mother immensely, but she admired the Duchesse d'Ambrée still more.

'*Maman baisse un peu,*' she often said to her sister, with a little scornful smile. She knew that her mother was twenty-eight; to Blanchette that age seemed to be quite hopeless decrepitude.

'Yseulte,' she said, suddenly now, 'if you do not give me your silver prayer-book, I shall tell mamma about you and papa. *Dis donc, sois sage.* Give me the silver Hours.'

The silver prayer-book had belonged to a Marquise de Creusac, in the time of Louis Treize. It was adorned with illuminated letters, and the coronet and initials were set in opals on one side of the silver cover. Yseulte had been given the book by her grandmother on her death-bed; she used it always, and it was the object of Blanchette's desires.

'You know that I cannot give it you,' said Yseulte, gently. 'It was my grandmother's last gift; it is an heirloom.'

Blanchette looked up from under her yellow hair.

'You had better give it me. *Sois sage!*'

She had the same expression—half menace, half malice—that her father had had.

'I cannot,' repeated her cousin, 'I have told you so, dear, a hundred times. I should not have a moment's peace if I parted with that book.'

Blanchette said nothing more, but she made a wheel of herself on the school-room floor, as she had seen the boys do on the pavement in Paris. 'Comme on est bête! Comme on est bête!' she kept thinking in her shrewd little mind, as she stood on her wise little skull with all the dexterity of any street-boy.

Blanchette at ten years old had already resolved the problem of life with great simplicity; its solution seemed to her to consist in getting whatever you wanted by being detestable whenever you did not get it.

On the night of the ball, when the first carriages rolled up to the *perron* of Millo, Yseulte, who had gone to bed at ten o'clock, but had not slept, rose and went to her window, which looked on the front of the house. The illuminations of the building and of the grounds were so brilliant that the light was almost as strong as day. The awnings hid from her sight the steps at which the arriving guests descended, but she could see the carriages as they came up toward them, and she could hear the Suisse bawl out the names of those who arrived one after another; amongst them some of the greatest names of Europe. At twelve she heard the name of Othmar; but she had not seen him, for the blinds of his brougham were down.

An hour and a half later, almost the last of the apparently endless succession of champing horses and lamp-lit coupés, she saw one carriage of which the window next her was lowered as it drove up; she could see within it a very lovely woman, with a little tiara of diamonds on her head, and a great bouquet, made entirely of gardenias, in her hand, and a cloak of gold tissue, lined with ermine, drawn up as high as her mouth. The lady's profile, delicate as if it were cut in ivory, with something satirical and mutinous in its expression, was all that Yseulte could see of her; but she felt that in that moment she had looked on the Princess Napraxine. In effect, as the carriage rolled beneath the awning, the sonorous Muscovite name was shouted by the waiting lackeys.

The girl withdrew from the casement and shut the shutters; she did not want to see any more.

She lay down again, but she did not sleep. The sound of dance music, played by the band of the ball-room, echoed through all the villa, which was a light modern structure, and had little solidity in it. She did not care for the dancing; she hardly knew what it was like; but she thought of the lovely woman with the pretty contemptuous profile, and the diamonds and the gardenias in her hair. She could not sleep for thinking of her; she was there below in the light, amidst the music and the flowers, and Othmar was there too. The visitants which Alain de Vannes had wished should go to her, envy and regret, entered her innocent soul, and made sad ravages there, as when a rat runs amidst a white rose and pulls its blossoms down.

Sleep kept aloof from her; she was ashamed of her own thoughts, but the dawn found her with hot wide-open eyes. The music was still sounding, like a tireless, immortal thing that shouted and laughed for its pleasure. It was only the first notes of the cotillon; but to Yseulte it sounded like the song of triumph of the world—that world which she would never know.

All her nuns and priests could not perhaps have read her a sounder homily than the house mutely spoke when she went timidly downstairs and through its many rooms at sunrise.

The flowers covering the balustrades and walls of the staircase were dying; the sleepy servants were turning out the gas, putting out the wax candles; other servants were drinking champagne and smoking cigars as they hurried to clear away the supper tables; in the ball-room there was a litter of dropped flowers, torn lace, discarded cotillon toys, atoms of fringe and of ribbon which looked scarcely better than rags; the torches were still flaming amongst the scorched clusters of azaleas and roses; in the vestibule two gentlemen who had stayed to drink some black coffee were putting on their furs and yawning miserably; Alain de Vannes, as he sauntered upstairs, was muttering, 'C'est crevant!—un bal chez soi:—on ne me reprendra jamais!'

and a maid of his wife's was recounting her griefs to a tall powdered lackey, with sobs of rage; 'Madame m'a donnée des gifles, mais des gifles!—enfin—elle tomba de sommeil et puis le petit Prangins n'a pas été gentil pour elle, du tout, du tout, ce soir!'

———————————

# CHAPTER XIII.

Nadine Napraxine meanwhile rolled home in the pale light of the winter morning, which had dawned over a quiet sea and a peaceful country. She was neither fatigued nor exhilarated by a ball which had been one of those long triumphs to which she was so well used. She looked as calm, as cool, as delicate of hue, as any Lenten lily that opens between the snow and the moss on an April morning. She was one of those women who can go through incredible fatigue, whether of pleasure or of travel, without any personal traces of it.

Whilst her companion, Lady Brancepeth, nodded and slumbered, she looked out at the landscape over which the sun was slowly dawning, driving before its rays the white mists which stretched over sea and mountain. There were people moving in it: women came down the steep stone ladders of their fields bearing heavy loads of oranges or of vegetables; mule carts plodded along the cactus-lined paths; fishermen were pushing boats into deep water; church bells were ringing. She, with her delicate and acute perception of what was beautiful, found pleasure in watching the simple hardy figures which were seen for a moment and then disappeared beneath the mist, in hearing the bells answer one another ringing across the white clouds that were touching the earth.

'What does it feel like,' she wondered, 'to sleep sound all night on a bit of sacking, and get up in the dusk, and go into the wet fields and labour? What do these people think about? What do sheep think about, or oxen? It must be much the same thing. Wilkes, what do field-labourers think about?—you have got ever so many at home, you ought to know.'

Lady Brancepeth felt cross at being aroused and cross at having been asleep:

'Think about?' she murmured; 'oh, I don't know; beer, I believe with us, beer and bacon; here I should say francs, nothing but francs, probably. What put them in your head? And there are no labourers here in our sense of the word, you know; it is most of it *la petite culture*, you know. I never believe it is good for the soil, certainly not in the long run; it can't be; they get everything out, they put nothing in. Of course they think only of the market of the day; they don't think of the future, those people. That will be always the upshot of peasant proprietors, they will always ruin the soil.'

Nadine Napraxine laughed:

'What a fine thing it is to be an Englishwoman; you think of political economy and of 'the soil' the very moment that you wake out of a doze! I suppose the earth will certainly last our time; what does the rest matter?'

'You are so—so—so egotistic and autocratic, Nadine.'

The Princess laughed:

'Oh, I don't know; I don't think so. I like a despotism, I was born under it; it saves so much trouble, and one big despot is very much easier to deal with than a score of little ones, especially when you stand well at his Court. It is always better to be judged by a judge instead of a jury, but simpletons will not see that.'

'But how can one judge, however just, rightfully judge a nation of millions unless he have the eyes and ears of Vishnou? I think you really are a despot by nature, but you are so very disputatious that you are always ready to repudiate your most cherished opinions for sheer sake of argument. You should have been a sophist.'

'Every question is polygonal. Look at that gleam of light on that sail and all the rest of the vessel lost in fog—how charming!—it is like a picture of Aïvanoffsky's. That is what I like in life; nothing said out, nothing broadly and rudely done, everything *à demi mot*, everything suggestion, not assertion; that is the only way to exhaust nothing, not to be wearied.'

'You like impressions, not pictures; that is the new school. Everyone is not satisfied with it. That there are people to whom these vague wavy lines, those dim washes of colour, tell little——'

'Oh, the people to whom one must explain! Let them all go where the sheep of Panurge went.'

'I wish you would condescend for once to explain something,' said Lady Brancepeth, and paused: Princess Nadine heard with a look of infinite *ennui*.

'You mean to revenge yourself for having been awakened out of that dose. I never explain—*enfin!*——tell me what you want.'

Under this slight encouragement Lady Brancepeth gained courage to plunge straightway into a question which she had long meditated.

'Will you tell me, my dear Nadine, what you mean to do with my brother?'

Madame Napraxine turned a little round in her ermine and gold brocade, and looked solemnly in her companion's face.

'My dear Evelyn, you amaze me! Do with him? I? With your brother?— with Lord Geraldine? What should I do with him? Do you want me to make a good marriage for him? But you are there to preside over that; and, besides, he will make one himself—some day.'

'Speak seriously for a moment,' said Lady Brancepeth with impatience. 'You are very clever, and are fond of *demi-mots*; I am a blunt, stupid woman, and so I like plain ones. It is two years since Geraldine has had any other thought than yourself. When will you be merciful and unmagnetise him?'

'Does that depend on me?' said the Princess Nadine, with a little laugh. 'Do you want me to make a few passes in the air with my hand? I can do it if you wish, but I doubt the result.'

Lady Brancepeth made an impatient movement.

'Poor Ralph is only one amongst many, I know, my dear; but for that very reason surely you might spare him? You do not care the least little atom about him——'

'The least little! I am a Russian, but I do know that is not good English. I speak better English than you do.'

'You do everything admirably well. You are the most intelligent as you are the most interesting woman that I know; but you are also the most heartless,' answered Lady Brancepeth with some heat. 'I am not a prude; I can understand temptation and the weakness that cedes to it; I can understand love and the force that it may exercise, and I can forgive even its follies; but your kind of coquetry I cannot forgive. It is the exercise of a merciless power which is as chill as a vivisector's attitude before his victim. You have no sympathy or compassion; you have only a sort of cynical amusement in what you do; you make yourself the centre of a man's life with no more effort than you use that fan; the man is nothing to you, nothing on earth; but you destroy all his peace, all his future——'

'Dear Wilkes, do not be so tragic!' murmured Princess Napraxine, with a little yawn. 'I dislike tragedy; I never by any chance go to Perrin's when they play one. If men are fond of me—as you say——'

'As I say!' ejaculated Lady Brancepeth.

'As you say; it is merely because—as you wisely if ungrammatically observed—it is because I do not care the "least little atom" about any one of them. I should have exceedingly liked to care for Platon; it would have been something new; it would have agreed with my programme of life; it would have suited me in every way; but *n'aime pas qui veut*; who *could* care for Platon? Does anybody ever care for a good-natured, very big, and entirely uninteresting person who drinks brandy and grows bald?'

'You beg my question,' retorted Lady Brancepeth; 'you know very well that I am not talking of your husband.'

'Then you ought to be if you be not! You are a very immoral woman to recommend me to care for anybody else,' said the Princess with her soft, quiet little laugh, that was as pretty as the coo of a wood dove but by no means so harmless.

'You would exasperate a saint,' cried her companion.

'I never met one,' said Nadine. 'The nearest approach to one that I know is Melville, and I can put *him* out of temper.'

'I have no doubt you can,' said Lady Brancepeth; 'I think you would anyone; you do such immeasurable harm, and are all the while as demure as a rabbit, and as innocent-looking. My dear Princess, you are the cruellest woman that lives! Flocon de Neige they call you. They might much more appropriately call you Goutte de Morphine. You enervate, and you kill, and all the while, what do you care? You care no more than the morphia does.'

'Did the ball bore you too so dreadfully that you are so very unkind? A rabbit and morphia! Your similes are mixed, my dear. I am never a flirt; a flirt is a very vulgar thing. No man lives, I can assure you, who could say he ever had a word of encouragement from me. That is not at all my way.'

'No!' said Lady Brancepeth, bitterly, 'your way is merely to look at men and destroy them, and then laugh a little when they are spoken of: I never reproached you with ordinary coquetry; I reproach you with something much more subtle, arrogant, cold, and cruel. There is a gum of the East advertised which does not kill flies, only attracts them, so that they cling to it by millions, and hang there stupidly in a throng till they die. That gum is very like your power over your lovers; it is just as passive, just as deadly.'

'The gum and I were made as we are by nature. Blame nature. The men and the flies would do worse if they did not do that. And pray do not talk about my lovers; I have none.'

'You have no serfs in Russia, but you have moujiks; and it is still much the same thing, as far as their submission goes.'

'You are really too sarcastic, Wilkes. Was Cri-Cri's champagne bad? Surely not. But there must be something you have not digested. Perhaps it is the caviare sandwiches. Here we are, at home. Do go to bed and dream of your gum, your rabbit, and your bottle of morphine. None of these things can swim, but I, who am a combination of them, can; and I shall be swimming under your window whilst you sleep.'

The carriage stopped at the foot of the terrace of La Jacquemerille, and she descended, aided by Geraldine, who, with her husband, had arrived a few minutes earlier.

Lady Brancepeth hurried indoors, conscious, with the consciousness of thirty-five years, that the morning light was not becoming after a ball. Nadine Napraxine, with the equally conscious immunity of an exquisite complexion, and of that kind of beauty which is like a sea-shell, unwound the lace from about her delicate head, and paused in the doorway, looking seaward.

'I shall not go to bed,' she said, as the rays of the sunrise touched the gilded pinnacles and vanes of La Jacquemerille. 'I shall go and get into a peignoir, then breakfast, and then bathe. It is so stupid to go to bed when the sun is up. Platon, you look like a bear awaked before he has done hybernating. Did you not get sleep enough in de Vannes' *fumoir*?'

'I never get sleep enough,' replied Napraxine, good-humouredly but drowsily; 'and you do a very foolish thing if you stand there, Princess, in a frost, at seven o'clock, after five hours of the cotillon!'

'There is no frost; look at the geraniums; and I never take cold; that is not my malady at all; I am not so silly.'

Napraxine opened his sleepy eyes.

'When you cannot live in Russia because the tubercles on your lungs——'

'Dr. Thiviers is responsible for the tubercles. One is obliged to say something civil to get away from a Court. It is always safe to say one suffers with one's lungs; nobody can ask to look at them. Pray go to bed, and dream of Nirvana, if you know what it means.'

The Prince obeyed, and disappeared yawning. Geraldine remained, gazing at this elegant figure on the marble step, with its *sortie du bal* of ermine and gold silk folded about it, and the face with its hue of a white tea-rose, which could defy so surely the searching morning light.

She glanced at him in return, and laughed. 'How droll you look with your *claque* and your ulster; you are not harmonious with the landscape, my friend; and you look sulky. The ball seems to have disagreed with all of you; yet it was a very good ball, as balls go; it is impossible to give any variety to a ball. Balls and funerals, *ça se ressemble trop.*'

She drew the ermine over her pretty chin, the diamonds sparkled in her hair; the bouquet of gardenias swung in her hand. The eyes of Geraldine grew very sombre and covetous.

'I am sorry I am a blot on the scene,' he said, moodily. 'Englishmen are always unpicturesque. I stood still and gazed at you all night, but no doubt I only looked like a policeman or a fool——'

'Or both,' she murmured, with a smile.

He continued unheedingly, 'While your friend Othmar, who did precisely the same thing, looked, of course, to you and to everybody, like a Titian resuscitated.'

'Othmar is not especially like any Titian that I have ever seen,' said Madame Napraxine, 'but he knows how to stand with grace, which no Englishman ever did know yet. You are quite right; your people do not "compose" well, except when they are in the hunting-field, or playing some very rough game; but you need not *souffler* for compliments; you are very good-looking—in your way.'

'Thanks,' muttered Geraldine, in a tone which would have better suited an imprecation.

Othmar had not danced once with her; he had indeed only moved reluctantly through a *contre-danse* with his hostess; but the unerring instinct of jealousy made the envy of Geraldine fasten on him rather than on any other of the crowd for whom the ball at Millo had only meant Princess Napraxine.

'It is a little chilly,' said the Princess as she turned from the open door.

Geraldine caught her hand which held the fan: 'If you would but believe all that your life is to us, you would not run such mad risks as this raw cold fog after a ball! Had I been Platon, I would have carried you to your room by main force.'

The face of Nadine Napraxine grew very cold.

'You are not Prince Napraxine—happily for myself and yourself; and I do not like impertinences. Go and smoke, and recover your good manners.'

'You were kinder to me before Othmar came home!' said Geraldine, with injudicious reproach.

'You have *very* bad manners,' said the Princess calmly, as she gathered up her ermine and drew her flower-laden train over the little hall and up the staircase.

She smiled as she passed upward.

'How babyish they all are!' she reflected. 'As if to complain of another man were not the very way to cement a woman's preference for him,—if she had any preference. That poor boy has no tact; if his sister had not said anything about him I would send him away; he is a bore. To be sure, he is here to take Platon off one's hands, and smoke with him. All men are tiresome when you have known them a month or so; all human beings are tiresome. Nobody ever tires of me, and I tire of everybody. Perhaps——'

She remembered that Othmar had alone never tired her; he had been too romantic, too presuming, too prone to fancy he had rights and wrongs; but he had never wearied her. Most men were so absurd when they were enamoured of her, but he was not so; a little too, like Ruy Blas perhaps a little too inclined to be serious and impassioned, to the *vieux jeu* in a word; but still he had kept his grace and kept his dignity. He kept them still; he would not let her play with him. She was the one woman on earth for him; but he did not become her slave.

She had her bath and wrapped herself in a loose gown of satin and lace and went out into the garden with a rose-coloured hood over her head. It was certainly cold, and the mists had not altogether cleared; but it was a point of honour with her to do what her physician and her friends denounced as most dangerous.

'Platon is snoring,' she thought contemptuously, as she glanced over the closed shutters. 'And I dare say Geraldine snores too, if one only knew. I dare say they both took soda and brandy. Men are certainly unlovely creatures. As long as we are young we are a little better than they; we look pretty asleep, and we don't snore. How *maquillée* poor Cri-Cri was last night, and then she really throws her heart into the affair with de Prangins; nothing ever ages a woman like that; and I am quite sure he does not care a straw about her.'

She walked up and down her terrace, trailing her rose-coloured skirts over the marble; she was a little sleepy, a little bored; but she wished to show to her friends that she could dance all night and breakfast out of doors without more fatigue than a nightingale, after singing all night, feels as he trips across the grass at sunrise.

She thought, with a little amusement, that, if Geraldine were really as wasting with despair as he professed to be, he would have been out of bed still on the mere chance of her reappearance. The various degrees of passions in her lovers diverted her; she had no vanity; she could dissect and weigh their emotions with perfect accuracy and philosophise upon them with a clearness of understanding wholly beyond the reach of vain woman. Analysis diverted her much more than conquest. Some had loved her tragically, some had died through her if not for her; she had had genuine triumphs, great enough and costly enough to satisfy the pride of anyone; therefore she could amuse herself very well with the contradiction when somebody, who declared that he only lived for her, nevertheless drank his claret with relish; or somebody else, who was for ever at her feet, nevertheless ceased not to be critical of his cigars.

'Poor Othmar!' she thought now; 'he would stay sleepless in the street all night on the chance of seeing my shadow on a window blind!'

That was the *vieux jeu*, romanticism which did not suit their world; which even made her impatient of it as indifferent people are always impatient of earnestness. But it was fine after all: finer than Geraldine's sulkiness which let him go to sleep.

The air was very cold, but the morning was fair, and the mists were lifting higher and higher every moment; as her skirts brushed the bay hedge it gave forth a sweet odour, snowdrops and hepatica blossomed under the big aloes, and ground ivy was green about the stems of the palms; the mountains grew the hue of summer roses under the sun's approach, then paled into amethyst and pearly grey; it was intensely quiet, there was no sound but of some unseen gardener sweeping up dead leaves; the yellow wings of an oriole flashed among the glossy leaves of a pitosperum.

'The world looks as if God washed it clean every morning,' she thought. 'It gets soiled before noon. Decidedly it is only the birds who are innocent enough for the sunrise.'

The latent sadness of the Russian character was in her, beneath her *insouciance* and her pessimism and her irony: sometimes she wished she had not been born to that world in which she lived, where there is no pause for reflection, but only a continuous succession of spectacles, excitations, revelries, where no one is ever alone, where no one has ever time to note a wild flower grow or a sun sink to the west, where the babble of society is for ever on the ear, and Nature has no place at all except as a *décor de théâtre* of which no one thinks more than the actor thinks of the painted canvas behind him with its bridge or its garden or its windmill.

'I do believe I should have liked to have been a poor woman and have married such a man as Millet or Corot,' she thought to herself now as she walked along the alley of bay that ran parallel with the sea. Then she laughed at the idea of herself, living in a cottage in a French wood, without any lace, without any diamonds, without any toilettes, looking for a dusty footsore artist coming home through the trees to his *pot au feu*. Somehow the artist in her fancy had the features of Othmar,—of Othmar, who was a prince of the Bourses and could no more escape the world than she could!

It scarcely surprised her when she saw him in person, as though her thoughts had compelled him to come thither. He was alone, in a little boat, which drifted slowly past the sea-terrace of La Jacquemerille; his hands rested idly on the oars, and his eyes were looking upward at the house.

She leaned down through one of the openings of the wall of clipt bay, and thrust her rose satin hood over the water:

'Is it you, Othmar?' she said to him. 'What are you doing on the sea at eight o'clock? How astonished you look! Do you wonder what I am doing in the open air? They are all asleep comfortably, though they think I am courting death. Row to the stairs; you can breakfast with me.'

He hesitated, looking up at her with his head uncovered and his eyes dazzled by the delicate face that was peering forth from the framework of close-sheared bay boughs.

'Come!' said Madame Napraxine. Her voice could be very imperious, and was so now.

He obeyed in silence, passed to the landing-place a hundred yards farther down, and in five minutes' time approached her under the arched roof of the bay charmille.

'But you were only back from the ball an hour or less!' he said, as he bowed before her.

'I was not inclined to go to bed; the morning is fine. You are up betimes, too. When did you leave Millo?'

'I left when you did,' said Othmar, with significance in the brevity of the reply.

'Then you cannot have breakfasted either. You will breakfast with me; I was just going back to the house.'

It was precisely the sort of *coup de scène* which would amuse her; her husband and Geraldine lounging downstairs, late, cross, and easily ruffled, to find her alone with their neighbour from S. Pharamond. It was one of those amusing little incidents which Providence, who, she was sure, was kind to her, was always sending her to relieve the monotony of human life.

'What were you doing under the sea wall?' she pursued. 'Is it your habit, too, never to go to bed? You must have been rowing some time. We are two sea leagues at least from your place. What did you think of Cri-Cri's ball? That new figure with the coloured hoops was pretty; but the Duc leads a cotillon better than anyone.'

'Admirable pre-eminence!' said Othmar. 'I saw you with the coloured hoops. You made them look as if Ariel had just brought them from Titania. But I do not think the charm was in the hoops themselves.'

'If you had cared to lead a cotillon, Othmar, you might have been a happier man.'

'That I do not doubt; the frivolous faculty is a very happy one.'

'At all events, though you despise it, you are indulgent to it. You gave us superb presents at your own fête. Come in to breakfast. I would not admit it if Platon were here, but it *is* cold.'

'And surely it is not very wise to be in the cold after a ball?'

'That is what they all said, so I came. I have not much sympathy with children, but I do understand why they like to do a thing for no other reason than that they are told not to do it. My physicians pretend that morning air is as bad as damp shoes, but I believe they say that to be agreeable to their patients who turn night into day. It is not only Molière's doctors who are charlatans. I imagine it is the perpetual affectation of sympathy which doctors are compelled to put on which makes them hypocrites. Come into the house.'

He went on in silence beside her along the bay path. He could not easily talk of trifles with her; she had filled all his life for two whole years; he loved her as he had loved no other woman. When he had returned home from the Millo ball, he had bathed and swam in the little bay of S. Pharamond, and then had rowed himself along the coast in that vague irresistible desire to pass near where she dwelt which every true lover feels.

He had resolved to emancipate himself from her power; as he had watched her through the night he had told himself that to care for her was to waste life on a baseless and ungrateful dream. Yet, when she had looked down from her evergreen rampart, and had said 'Come,' he had been unable to resist.

As he paced beside her now, the delicate perfume of her laces, the floating, indefinite lines of the rose-satin draperies, the glimpse of her profile which the hood showed, her slender feet in their rose-coloured pearl-sewn slippers, which stepped so lightly over the shining shingle of the paths— one and all they conquered his calmness and his resolves, as the fumes of new wine mount over the brain and move the senses. She walked on, provocative as Venus, unattainable as Una, speaking idly of this thing and of that, knowing very well what made his answers all at random and his colour changeful. Other women might need to use all the arts of conquest; might need to woo with their eyes, to charm with their smiles, to solicit with their glances. She had no such vulgar fashions; she moved, spoke, looked, as the moment actuated her, and noticed her lovers hardly more than she noticed the little dog that ran after her skirts. To exist and to be seen was enough to secure her more victories than she chose to count.

If she noticed Othmar more than others it was because he had gone away from her, he had rebuked her, he had appeared to defy her, and he had dared to tell her he loved her with more reproach, and more bitterness of soul than any other had ever done. She did not intend to accept his life, or to give him hers; but she did intend that his should be unable to detach itself. And all the while she talked to him with that easy, even kindness, as of a friend, with those light philosophies of a woman of the world, which were to the passions of a man as ether spray thrown upon a lava-flood; and she took him into breakfast with her as though he were her brother.

She occasionally drank her chocolate in a boudoir opening on to the terrace; a little nest of white satin and looking-glass and Saxe china; the ceiling was a mirror painted with little doves and flowers; the carpet was of lambskins; the corners were filled with azaleas, rose and white, like her gown. She looked only a larger flower as she sank down on one of the couches. The chocolate was served on Moorish trays, in Turkish cups, by a little negro who, gorgeous in his dress and immovable as a statue, was often taken by new comers for an enamelled bronze cast by Barbédienne, so motionless did he squat before the door of any room she occupied. Othmar almost envied that little African menial the right he had to see his mistress pass and repass a hundred times a day. Nadine, in her nonchalant way, was kind to the boy.

'He will die of pneumonia,—they always do,' she said now. 'Poor dusky little beetles, they only live by their hot sand and their hot sun; to be sure, our houses inside are as hot as Africa, but outside, the east wind blows, and one day it will blow too much for Mahmoud. I suppose it would be a terrible thing for civilisation if the East ever again surged over the West; but the East has very much to avenge, and I am not sure that civilisation would be any great loss. It has discovered that man is only a sort of hotbed for bacteria, and that butter can be made out of river mud, and coffee out of powdered tan.'

She had taken the hood off her head; she was as charming as a child freshly out of a bath, with her eyes brilliant and her cheeks a little warmed by the transition from the chill air of early morning to the room heated to 30° Réaumur. She had tossed herself backwards amongst the white satin cushions. Her eyes, which were like onyx, dwelt on him with a gleam of amusement; her beautiful mouth had the smile which was so enigmatical, so gay, and yet so cold. She had had a different smile when she had said to little Mahmoud, 'Cover yourself warmly here; though the sun shines, it is not African.'

'What has that black brat done that you are so merciful to him?' asked Othmar.

She replied: 'That black brat is a victim of civilisation. I hate civilisation, as you know. It even adulterates truffles.'

'Did you ever smile so kindly on your own children?'

'I cannot say. I do not count my smiles. That poor little slave is interesting, he is an exile, and he will die in a year or two; my children are insufferably uninteresting; they have unchangeable health, intense stupidity, and will grow up to have every desire fulfilled, every caprice gratified, and to become that irresponsible, useless, tyrannical, anachronism—a Russian noble. Perhaps they will be good soldiers and kill a score of Asiatics. Perhaps they will only drink brandy, and gamble.'

Othmar did not reply; he was looking at the exquisite grace of her form, the tea-rose tint of her cheeks. Was it possible that she could be the mother of two stout, ugly, Tartar-faced boys? It seemed to him a profanation; a hideous incongruity. He did not like to think of it. If she had had a child at all it should have been some blossom-like creature, sharing her own grace as the catkin shares the willow's. The subtlest charm about her was that ethereality, as of a virginal goddess, which was blent in her with all the *finesses* of seduction and of mind. The boldest man felt that in Nadine Napraxine the senses had hardly more empire than in the ivory Venus of the Greeks.

The eyes of Othmar dwelt on her now yearningly, sombrely, wistfully.

'It is of no use,' he said, abruptly. 'I did wrong to come here. If you wish for men who can, whilst they adore you, sit and drink chocolate and talk epigrams, seek elsewhere; I am not one of them. I can wear a mask, but it must be of iron, not of velvet.'

'The iron mask was of velvet,' said she, correcting him, unmoved by the repressed passion in his voice. 'All our illusions vanish under the electric light of history, and the iron mask is one of them. I daily expect to hear that Marie Antoinette was never guillotined, but succumbed at seventy to dropsy at Schönbrunn; we know it is proved that Jeanne d'Arc married and died, *bonne bourgeoise*, at Orleans, and her family enjoyed a pension for three generations from the town. It is very distressing, but it is all proved from the archives. Why shouldn't you drink chocolate? Perhaps you do not like it. Men like nothing that has sugar in it, except flattery. Ring. They will bring you anything else.'

Othmar looked at her without speaking. Something of the impotent rage against her with which he had left her in Paris awoke in him under the sting of her ever dulcet tones, in which a little tone of mockery could be felt rather than heard.

He rose abruptly.

'Have you never loved anyone?' he asked.

She lifted her eyebrows with impatience and astonishment.

'*Vous voila emballé!* Dear Othmar, I should like you so much if you would not always revert to that old theme. You are a man of the world, or you ought to be one. Be amusing, even be instructive if you like; I do not mind being instructed, but do not be romantic. Nobody is nowadays; not even the novelists.'

Othmar appeared scarcely to hear her.

'Did you never love anyone?' he repeated.

She laughed a little.

'You speak as if I were forty years old, with a cabinet full of old letters and faded roses! No; I never loved anybody, not even Platon!'

The notion suggested in her last words tickled her fancy so much that she laughed outright.

'I suppose,' she continued, 'somewhere in the world there are women who have loved Platon; but it seems too funny. He is always eating when he is not drinking; he is always smoking when he is not sleeping; *admettons, donc,* that Cupid must fly from his presence. How grave you look. I believe you have something of the Eastern in you, and think that all women should be prostrate before their husbands. There is a good deal of that idea among the moujiks; it must be very agreeable—for the man.'

'Why did you marry him?' said Othmar, gloomily; it hurt his sense of honour to speak of Napraxine in Napraxine's house; yet he could not repress the question.

'Oh, my friend, why do girls always marry?' she said, indifferently. 'Because the marriage is there; because the families have arranged it; because one does not know; because one wishes for freedom, for jewels, for the world; because one does not care to be a *fillette,* chaperoned at every step. There are many reasons that make one marry: it is the thing to do—everyone does it; when a girl sees the young married women, she sees them flirted with, sought, monopolising everything; it is like standing behind a shut door and hearing people laughing and singing on the other side, while you cannot get to them; besides, Platon did as well as anybody else, he is more good-natured than most; he never interferes; he is very peaceable——'

'How long ago is it? Five years—six? Why could I not meet you before?'

She smiled, not displeased.

'It is seven years. Oh, I do not think it would have done at all; you are too arrogant; we should have quarrelled before a month was out. Besides, I should have tormented you to do all manner of impossibilities; with your immense power, I should have expected you to buy me an empire.'

Othmar was very pale; the possibility of which she jested so airily was one he could not think of without a mist before his eyes, a quickening of his heart. He hesitated to say what rose to his lips; she would only call it *vieux jeu*.

'I think you might be a great man, Othmar, if you were not Othmar,' she pursued.

'I do not feel the capabilities,' he replied.

'That is because you are what you are,' she answered. 'You are something like a king of England. A king of England might have all the talents, but he could never be a great man because his position binds him hand and foot, and makes a lay figure of him. You are not a lay figure, but the very fact that you are Otho Othmar prevents your being anything besides. I think, if I were you, I should buy some great sunshiny fantastic eastern kingdom, and reign there; you might lead the life of a Haroum Alraschid, and forget all about our stupid Europe with its big dinners, its blundering politics, its unreal religions, and its hideous dress.'

'A charming dream—if you were with me.'

'Oh, no; you would not want me; you would have two thousand slaves, each more beautiful than the others.'

'All my life I shall want you!'

He spoke under his breath. He was leaning back in his chair; his face was cold, almost stern, but his eyes were ardent and full of passion. All night at Millo he had sworn to himself that never again would he succumb to her influence or allow her to triumph in the power she possessed over him, but in her presence he was unnerved, and unable to keep silent. She, lying back amongst her cushions, glanced at him under her long lashes, and understood very well the strife which went on in his soul; the pride of manhood which combatted the impulses of passion; the impetus which could not be resisted, the impatience of his own weakness which vibrated through his confession.

'What was the use of your going to Mongolia; you could not escape *me*,' she thought, with a little of that contemptuous indulgence which she always felt for her lovers' follies, and a little of a newer and more personal gratification; for Othmar touched a certain chord in her mind, a certain pulse in her heart, which others had not done. There was nothing commonplace or trivial in him. There was a vague power, unused but existent, which commanded her respect. Nadine Napraxine despised the world too heartily herself not to have sympathy with the indifference he felt for his own potentialities and possessions. He was one of the masters of the world, and he only wished for one thing on earth—herself. There was a flattery in that which pleased even her, sated with compliment though she was. There were moments when she thought that if she had met him before, as he said, there would have been less ennui and more warmth in her life. 'Only we should have been so sure to have tired of each other,' she reflected. 'People always do; it is the fault of marriage; it compels people at the onset to see so much of one another that they have nothing new left with which to meet the future. If you heard the best of Bach every day, you would get to hate Bach as intensely as you hate a street organ; the music would still be perfect, but it could not withstand incessant repetition. We should have been quite idylically in love for a few months; I am sure we should; but then we should have each gone our several ways, and in the end he would have been hardly better than Platon.'

Aloud, however, she only said, with a little smile:

'You should never say things straight out like that, Othmar. You should never go beyond a suggestion. The world has spoilt you so greatly that it has let you get blunt. It is a pity. When I talk to people I always feel as Boucher said he felt when he talked with his lady-love. "J'aime tout ce qu'elle va dire; je n'aime rien qu'elle dit." If we could only always remain at the stage when we are just going to speak!'

Othmar did not reply. His face was very pale; it had a set stern look, as though he exercised great self-repression. He was angered against himself for being there; for having let her lead him thither merely to be made the sport of her subtle and sarcastic intelligence. It seemed to him that if his passion were unwelcome to her his presence should be unwelcome too.

She guessed his thoughts with that rapid intuition which is the gift of such minds as hers.

'Oh, I am not like that,' she said, with some unspoken amusement; 'I am not startled at a confession like yours, as a horse starts at a pistol shot. It seems to me that men are never happy unless they are talking in that kind of way to some woman who does not belong to them. They are so like children! In Petersburg, last year, I saw Sachs crying for a sentinel's cartouche-box because he could not have it. He had all Giroux's shop in his own nursery, but that did not do. You are like Sachs. Ought I to ring the bell and dismiss you? Why should I? I do not think so. Only very primitive beings take fright at declarations. Besides, you made me so many in Paris, and then you went to the Mongols. I never knew why you went to the Mongols; why did you go?'

'Wounded brutes always get away somewhere to be unseen as long as their wound bleeds,' said Othmar, with some bitterness.

'How Sachs cried for that cartouche-box!' she said, as she lit a cigarette. 'His women scolded him, but I said to them, "Why do you scold him? He is a male creature; therefore he must weep for what he cannot get." Some children cry for the moon; a moon, or a cartouche-box, or a woman, the principle is the same.'

Othmar rose and approached her. He seemed scarcely to have heard her jest.

'Nadége, hear me a moment,' he said, in a low tone, through whose enforced calmness there was the thrill of an intense passion. 'You are not alarmed at declarations; they are nothing to you, you neither requite nor reject them; they amuse you, that is all. You are used to do just what you please with men; I understand that you despise them so far as you deign to think of them seriously.'

'Despise, no!' she said, with a little gesture of depreciation; 'that is too strong. Why should I despise them for acting according to their natures? I do not desire cartouche-boxes myself, but I did not despise Sachs.'

'I told you in Paris,' pursued Othmar, 'that I would not add one to the list of those whom you have made ridiculous in the eyes of the world. I will be all to a woman, or nothing to her. You would have let me swell the cortège that marks your triumphal passage; you would have let me fill the place that Lord Geraldine occupies now. You would have allowed me to drive with you, dine with you, come in and out of your house, take your husband away when he bored you, do everything that Lord Geraldine is permitted to do now; and you would have repaid me as you repay him, by a little laugh, a smile now and then, a vague liking which would have grown, little by little, into contempt! I would not accept that place in your household. I would not then. I left you, though it cost me more than you would ever know or pity, for you do not understand what love is. I went away; I desired to escape from you. I did escape. I desired also to forget you, but I could not forget. You are not a woman who can be forgotten; you are like one of those *miséricordes* with which they stabbed men in the Valois days, that look like mere threads of silver sheathed in velvet, and yet can go home through breast and bone, and kill more surely than swords that are as high as a man's shoulder——'

He paused a moment; he breathed quickly and heavily; she looked up, holding her little cigarette suspended:

'I am like a great many things,' she murmured; 'I thought Wilkes exhausted all possibilities in comparison this morning. Go on! you are very *entreprenant*, but it rather becomes you; you may go on if you like.'

He dropped on his knee beside her:

'No, I would not be what Geraldine is; you tolerate him now, to scorn him immeasurably hereafter. His own weakness will be the measure of your scorn. He has never dared to say to you what I said to you in Paris, what I say now: love me, or I will not see your face again, except as society may compel me to see it in a crowd. Listen, Nadine! I love you, only you; I never thought to love any woman so; but I love you as men did in the old times, and there is nothing I will not surrender to you save my own self-respect. If to meet you, to touch your hand, to hear your voice, I must come and go like a dog in your husband's house, petted one day, chidden the next, absurd in my own sight and emasculated in the sight of others, I will wrench my love for you out of my life if my life goes with it! Last night I heard someone who did not know him inquire who Geraldine was; someone else answered him, "Oh, that is one of Princess Napraxine's *ensorcelés*; she never looks at him, but he is content to follow her shadow." You know me very little if you believe I would ever let the world speak of me like that. I told you in Paris I would never be the trembling valet of a bloodless Platonism!'

She looked at him, and a gleam of admiration passed into her eyes for a moment; she breathed a trifle more quickly; she thought to herself: 'He is superb when he looks and speaks like that! *C'est un homme celui-là!*

She did not speak, she leaned back amongst her cushions with a little look of expectancy upon her face; the whole thing pleased her, as some admirable piece of acting on the boards of the Théâtre Français pleased at once her eye, her ear, and her taste.

But Othmar was passionately in earnest; all his heart was in his lips, all his passions had found voice. He could scarcely see her for the red mist that swam before his eyes, for the tumult of his senses. He dropped on his knee beside her.

'Nadine,' he murmured, as his forehead touched her hand, 'I have told you what I will not do; let me tell you what I will do. I will do as you say, I will buy some sunlit kingdom far away in the heart of Asia, and I will take you to it and obey every breath of your mouth as my one divine law. I will turn my back on Europe once and for ever; I will let men call me a coward, a fool, an infidel; what they will; I will give all my present and all my future to you and to you alone; all I possess shall only exist to minister to you; I will be your slave, body and mind and will; but only *so*—only if you give yourself to me as absolutely in return, only if you come with me where nothing of this world which we have known shall pursue us to remind me that you were ever else than mine.'

His forehead burned her hand as it touched her, his voice was passionate in its emotion and eloquence, his heart beat so loudly that it was audible in the stillness around them. For once she was touched, almost awed; for once the electricity of the passion she excited communicated something of its fire and thrill to her. She was silent a few moments, her eyelids closed, her lips parted, she felt a vague pleasure in the contact of this intense and imperious love. He saw upon her delicate features a change of colour, a flicker of emotion, which no one else had ever seen there; but she motioned him farther away from her with that dislike to any concession and that sensitive hauteur which but added to her charm.

She smiled a little, but there was an accent which was almost tenderness in her voice as she said to him: 'C'est de ne rien perdre de beaucoup prier! You evidently have belief in that saying. It is to ask a very great deal, but then you would give a great deal in your turn. Go away now; I will think. No, I shall not answer you; I want time for thought. Be satisfied that I am not offended, and go. I ought to be so, I suppose, but I am not. Go.'

'I may come back?'

His heart beat eagerly and exultantly. He was not refused or dismissed! 'Château qui parle, femme qui écoutee'—the old proverb drifted through his thoughts, all confused as they were in a tumult of hope and desire, and triumph and doubt. A moment's hesitation from her was more concession than a thousand caresses from a humbler woman.

'I may come back?' he repeated, as she remained silent.

'If you like, we shall meet in other places; yes, you may return in a fortnight—at this time—in this room, then I will tell you.'

'In a fortnight!'—it seemed to him to be ten years.

'Be thankful for so much,' she said, as she gave him the tips of her fingers. 'Now go. Mahmoud is in the antechamber.'

He kissed her hand with lips that burned like fire, bowed low and obeyed her. Nadine Napraxine remained motionless, her eyes were closed, her mouth smiled; she seemed to dream.

THE END OF THE FIRST VOLUME.

Milton Keynes UK
Ingram Content Group UK Ltd.
UKHW030719041024
449263UK00004B/380

9 789362 096395